150TH GREAT JONES COUNTY FAIR 2002

FIVE BEST DAYS of Summer

GREAT JONES COUNTY FAIR

Elinor Day

Published by WDG Publishing

GREAT
JONES COUNTY
FAIR
NIGHT CARNIVAL
MONTICELLO
AUGUST
21-25

FIVE BEST DAYS of Summer
150th GREAT JONES COUNTY FAIR · 2002

Elinor Day

Published by WDG Publishing

150th Great Jones County Fair

Five Best Days of Summer

Creative Direction	Duane Wood
Design/Art Direction	Eric C. Johnson
Production Management	Shari Boyle
Cover Illustration	William Ersland

Copyright © 2002 WDG Publishing

First published in the United States of America by
WDG Communications Inc.
3500 F Avenue NW
Post Office Box 9573
Cedar Rapids, Iowa 52409-9573
Telephone (319) 396-1401
Facsimile (319) 396-1647

Library of Congress Cataloging-in-Publication Data

Day, Elinor, 1927-
    Five best days of summer : 150 years of the Great Jones County Fair /
by Elinor Day.
        p. cm.
    ISBN 0-9651620-8-7 (alk. paper)
1. Great Jones County Fair--History. I. Title
    S555.I8 D38 2002
    630′ .74777′63--dc21
                                        2002004754

Printed in the United States of America

10 9 8 7 6 5 4 3 2 1

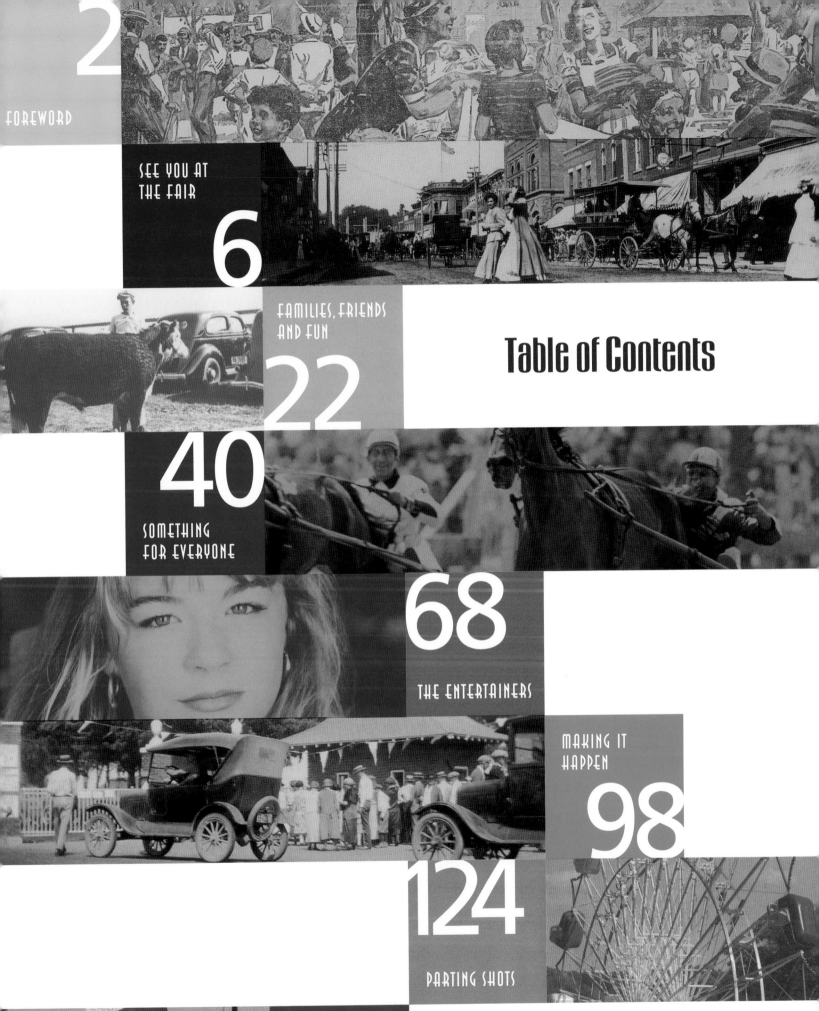

Table of Contents

Grab a cup of something to sip on, nestle into your favorite easy chair, and let's visit.

FOREWORD

Name all the things you can think of that are 150 years old. What do they have in common? Solid foundations, strong and durable construction materials, appropriate locations, proper maintenance, and the sheer desire to keep them standing, to name just a few. These characteristics describe permanent structures, and many of us will have named historic buildings, monuments, and the like.

Now shift your thoughts a little and try to think of a business or an event that has been alive for 150 years. How many of those come to mind?

The Great Jones County Fair is one of those rare traditions that have endured, through good times and bad. We celebrate the 150th annual Fair in 2002, which is also the 100-year celebration of the founding of 4-H.

The logic behind the Fair's long duration is familiar. Solid foundations with strong and durable construction materials:

Agriculture. The fundamental basis of the fair system is agriculture — all aspects of it. These roots are solid, and must never be forgotten if the true meaning of the fair or exhibition is to endure.

Location and maintenance. The Fairground facility is one of the most beautiful sites in the country. It is a well-manicured city park used year-round, overlooking a beautiful golf course and the Maquoketa river. Easily accessed from US Highway 151 and Iowa Highway 38, the 200-acre facility has parking for 10,000 cars and room for growth.

Desire to continue. The most important key to the longevity and future success of the Fair is the people. We are extremely fortunate to have people who want to make it happen: the boards, the volunteers, the concessionaires,

THE MONTICELLO EXPRESS

SECTION TWO

VOLUME LXXIV · Each For All And All For Each. · MONTICELLO, IOWA, AUGUST 11, 1938. · Subscription Price $2.00 · NUMBER 5

IOWA *Centennial*

AND THE CELEBRATED

GREAT JONES COUNTY

85th ANNUAL

FAIR

4 Big Nights

3 Big Days

Monticello Iowa

AUGUST 23 TO 26

Thursday, August 25 will be "COUNTY DAY" at the Fair

Six Heats of Harness Racing Every Day

the entertainers, the youth, the yearly patrons.
This county fair provides unlimited satisfaction
for those who take part. I am humbled to be
a small part of this enduring tradition.

We are excited to share some of the moments
in the rich history of the Great Jones County
Fair in this commemorative volume. So put
your feet up, take another sip, and enjoy the
Five Best Days of Summer.

John Harms
General Manager

At dusk,
the Midway
becomes a
magical place.

There's a buzz in the early morning air. Youngsters are washing down their livestock. Crews are readying the grounds. The sun comes up on the celebration everyone has been waiting for: *the Five Best Days of Summer.*

SEE YOU AT THE FAIR

"I can't remember not going to the Fair. That was our vacation. You forgot about your farm work for a few days and went to the Fair. You always met a lot of people and made a lot of new friends. I grew up at the Fair," says Marilyn Streeper of Anamosa.

Marilyn isn't alone. By now — with 150 years of history — there are thousands of people who "grew up" at the Great Jones County Fair. They came wrapped in blankets, snuggled in their parents' arms. They came to race their tricycles. They came to show their heifers, demonstrate their sewing ability, try out the rides. They came to see the shows, eat the hamburgers, see their friends. And most of all, they came to have fun.

Families, friends and fun — that's what the Fair is all about. That concept hasn't changed in 150 years; it has just grown, like the Fair itself.

Deeply rooted in agriculture, the Great Jones County Fair came into being in 1853 as a celebration of the harvest — a day for farm families to relax, to picnic, and to share and display their accomplish-

ments. It was held on Bowen's Prairie, mid-way between Monticello and Cascade. By 1857, however, the Fair had moved to Anamosa, and the Jones County Agricultural Society established permanent exhibition grounds there in 1859. The Fair flourished until the Civil War, when interest diminished. In succeeding years it was affected by rainy weather. Finally — in 1873 — it rained so much that the Fair was not held at all.

In 1874, a new organization became the sponsor of the Fair and moved it to Monticello. The Jones County Fair Association held the Fair that year on the grounds of the Union Driving Park Association, which were later sold to the city for a park. Anamosa reorganized a fair that competed with the Monticello Fair from 1879 until 1931.

During its earliest days, families came to the Fair in farm wagons, buggies, and on horseback. Writing in "Monticello, Iowa, 1836-1986," William Corbin notes that "Men still rode horseback and it was common to see people walking the roads and railroad tracks.

Many Fair events were held in tents in the 50s.

Horse-drawn wagons took people to the Fair in 1907.

Cars and buggies shared Monticello streets in 1908.

Special excursion trains brought people to the Fair in 1910.

Long dresses and hats were proper Fair attire in 1915.

Buggies were the popular means of traveling about the county. To supply wagons and buggies, Monticello had top skilled workmen and wagon shops which could build any type of vehicle desired."

By the 1870s the railroad tracks Corbin referred to had proliferated. "As the years passed," he writes, "large numbers of hogs, horses, and grain were brought into Monticello from area farms and shipped out by rail."

Passenger service also was important; Monticello had two railroads by 1872, with as many as 13 trains a day listed at the depot. One railroad was the Dubuque Southwestern (later sold to the Chicago Milwaukee & St. Paul Railroad), which served the towns of Dubuque, Farley, Worthington, Sand Springs, Junction Switch, Monticello, Langworthy, Anamosa, Stone City, Viola,

Springville, Paralta, Marion and Cedar Rapids.

Through the late 1800s and early 1900s, special excursion trains brought people to the Fair. Among the improvements made for the 1883 Fair was a sidewalk from the depot to the Fairgrounds, a favor to the ladies who complained of having to walk through mud and dust in their long skirts.

Writing the history of the Fair for its centennial observance in 1953, Gail McNeill tells us:

"Fair week of 1909 was decidedly damp, still excursionists braved the elements to arrive from north and south. The Davenport Band, which had been hired for the Fair, met each train at the depot. The crowds were so great that the band was pushed back into the depot park, where the iron fountain bubbled and frothed,

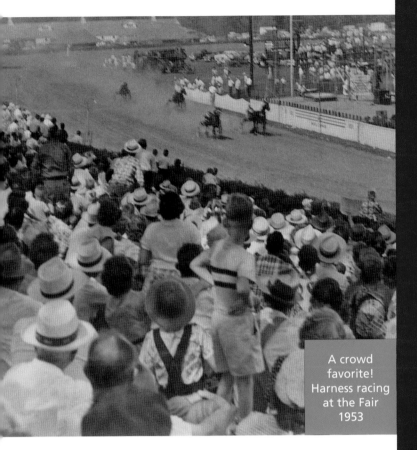

A crowd favorite! Harness racing at the Fair 1953

Pedal Pushers and Lipstick

When I lived in Monticello, which was for 18 years, the Fair was always in August. All year long I saved quarters in a glass jar that was shaped like a bear (I suppose honey was in the jar when it was purchased) so that I would have plenty of money to spend at the Fair.

My dad, Tom Eden, was on the Fair board, and was given some free passes, which he gave to me, so with my quarters, I always had plenty of money to spend; however, I do recall now and then hitting him up for more, and he never refused, but would hand me a five-dollar bill.

Dad raced his harness horses in Monticello, and one year he let me lead the horses onto the track before a race. What a thrill it was for me! I dressed in a black and white Mexican outfit and rode our riding horse, Toby. Dad's colors were purple and white. Often I would go into the tack room at the barn and listen to the horsemen tell tall tales of previous races, and enjoy the aroma of their cigars.

Dressing for the Fair was an important thing. During the day, we wore short shorts or pedal pushers, as they were called then, and starched blouses and *lipstick*. At night, we wore full skirts with cancans under them and starched blouses and a sweater, and *lipstick*.

Cars were given away then, as they weren't as expensive as they are today. You could hear a pin drop as everyone waited to see whose name would be called for each drawing.

With wonderful memories, I want to say "Happy Birthday" 150 years to the Great Jones County Fair.

Tammy Eden Huie
Locust Grove, Georgia

aided by the natural showers. Pressed by the crowds, a trombone player stepped back and tumbled into the fountain, where he continued to blow from among the iron mermaids."

The automobile eventually brought about the demise of short-run railroads and horse-drawn travel. In 1889, the Fair put in extra hitching posts; 20 years later, there were so many automobiles that latecomers had to drive to the east side of the track and park opposite the amphitheater. Passenger rail service to the Fair was reinstated, however, during World War II gas and tire rationing, when the Milwaukee Road adjusted its schedule to accommodate Cedar Rapids visitors.

Today, as many as 10,000 cars a day park on the

Fairgrounds. The Great Jones County Fair has grown to encompass many other interests and attractions, but agriculture still provides its foundation and its family orientation.

Generations of families have enjoyed the Fair together, in 4-H activities, as Fair volunteers, or simply by "coming back to Monticello" for the Fair. Jenny Myers is the fourth Fair-going generation in her family. Jenny lives in Cedar Rapids, as do her parents, John and Carol Myers. John's grandfather was Fred Kay, a Monticello druggist who served on the Fair board during the 1920s.(Kay's drug store was located

on the corner where the Big Dollar store is now.)

John has been going to the Fair since he was five years old. He and his brother, Bob, always visited their grandparents during Fair week. "I can still remember the twin beds we slept in, in the house on South Gill Street," John says. "Businesses used to shut down in the afternoons during Fair week. I guess some of them still do. I remember Grandpa taking me to the horse races — he had announced the races at one time — and the stage acts. After the evening performance, we'd go home and make big root beer floats.

"When I was a little kid, they had a clown act —

a really small car would drive around the stage. When it stopped, eight or 10 clowns would come out. They had to be coming through a trap door in the stage, but I was young enough that I didn't know that."

As he grew older, John's favorite Fair event was the stock car races. After he and Carol were married, they started camping out at the Fair, in a tent on the golf course. "Then we got a travel trailer," John says. "For years, there would be as many as 100 campers back there by the golf course. I used to take a week's vacation, and we'd take our kids. Now we camp at Walnut Acres. We leave our trailer there all summer and go back and forth."

Jenny goes, too. Like her dad, she "grew up" at the Fair. She hasn't missed one since she was six months old. "I used to watch them make cotton candy.

It was my favorite thing," she says.

John and Carol Myers have made many friends over the years, and look forward to seeing them at Fair time. "Every night, every year, year after year, we're here," says John. And Carol adds, "I don't know what it is — there's just something about the Jones County Fair."

What is that "something"? At least part of it, some people say, is the Fairgrounds. "I don't think you'll find a prettier fairground in the whole state," says Marilyn Streeper.

As a Fair board member and past president, Marilyn might be accused of being just a little biased — if so many others didn't agree with her. Varlyn Fink, retired 4-H youth director, is one who wholeheartedly supports her view. "Other fairgrounds are on the edge of their towns, weedy, with no shade. Because it is a

(Continued on page 14)

A Fair to Remember

My father, Leo Demmer, carries a picture in his billfold dated August 22, 1946. The picture was taken at the Jones County Fair when Leo, of Dyersville, went on a date with his girlfriend, Stella Goedken, of Petersburg. Leo and Stella were dressed in their church attire (they said back then you always dressed up when you went somewhere). They remember spending the day at the Fair, going on the rides, watching a baseball game and watching the harness racing.

Leo and Stella were married one year later. They now live in Dubuque, and have nine children, 28 grandchildren, and one great-grandchild.

On July 19, 2001, Leo and Stella had their picture taken once again at the Jones County Fair. This time they spent the day taking some of their grandchildren on the rides, watching their grandchildren show hogs, and watching the harness racing. It was a perfect way to re-live those memories from their date in 1946.

LuAnn Demmer Manternach
Cascade, Iowa

When the Fair Was Just For Me

Before cars had seatbelts or kids had computers, my sister Jana and I spent every Fair week with our Grandma Blanche and Grandpa Henry Adams in Monticello. We loved it. For a small town to cradle a magnificent entertainment giant that drew thousands of people was amazing, all the more because Monti was so unassuming the rest of the year.

Grandma, Grandpa and other relatives helped run the Lions Club stand. Fragrant of fried burgers and homemade pies, that brick food stand was the center of our universe at the Fair. Up to the right was the Jaycees stand where Uncle Jim toiled. To the left was

Summer,
best friends
and the Fair!

the hall where our cousins displayed their 4-H skills. Ahead and down the hill were the racetrack and the grandstand where Brenda Lee sang, Dave Nelson did a trapeze act and Charlie Weaver spun homey tales of Mt. Idy. Above that to one side was the beer tent where men stood drinking around a ring of metal troughs filled with water, bottles and ice.

My sister baked pies with Grandma and worked the Lions stand. I worked there too, but I lived to roam the Fair, from the stables on the north end to the sideshows on the south. I relished weaving among the fairgoers, playing a few games of ostensible chance and skill, riding the rides, soaking it all in. Once, after listening to a barker lustily entice men to enter the girlie show, my cousins and I slipped around back and peeked under the tent. As a carny chased us off, we laughed, thrilled by our daring.

As fun as it was to cruise the Midway after dark while the colored lights worked their magic, another fascinating time was early morning. Sometimes, before the Fair opened for the day, we'd come in to do prep work in the Lions stand. I'd wander off to explore. The roustabouts worked at night, so they slept late in trailers and trucks. Their existence seemed exotic. As I walked the uninhabited Fairground, the smells of the damp grass and trees mingled with the glorious unnaturalness of the Fair. I felt privileged, as if in those few moments the Great Jones County Fair was mine alone.

Kim Ketelsen
Marion, Iowa

Kids take an afternoon spin in the city park.

Volunteer Boy Scouts on the clean-up!

city park, the Jones County Fairground is used by the community. You'll see people on their lunch hours, children on swings, people playing on the ball diamonds and golf course — it was so wisely planned."

Add to that a grassy slope that forms a natural amphitheater, along with an exhibition hall that is a community center the other 51 weeks of the year. Then add a picnic shelter that is enclosed to serve as an exhibit hall one week of the year. Stir in a heavy helping of maintenance and improvements, and you have the recipe for an attractive and welcoming Fair setting.

Others say that beautiful grounds are only part of that certain "something." When you look at the number of people who are involved in planning and putting on the Fair, it's easy to see that another important element is community commitment.

It begins with an elected board representing all of the districts in the county, along with representatives from related entities and interests — city and county governments, the golf club, which own portions of the land and facilities, and county extension services. They serve without pay. They direct an enthusiastic part-time staff. They all work hard and they work long — a week after the Fair, they begin working on the following summer's Five Best Days.

About 200 more volunteers are involved the week before and during the Fair, selling tickets, baking pies, cleaning buildings, making sure everything is ready to go. The Boy Scouts are there every morning at six, picking up trash and restoring pristine order to the grounds. Helping to make it all possible are the hundreds of businesses and individuals who donate premiums and sponsorships.

A Favorite Fair Treat: Nutsticks

In 1948, Carl Schneider, manager of the Borden's Ice Cream branch in Monticello, asked Don Skelley if he would like to take over the ice cream stand at the Fair. Paul Schneider helped Don the first year, but after that Don recruited family to help him.

In 1950, Don started making nutsticks. He made them at the Korn Krib, a small confectionery store in Anamosa, and the Borden's delivery man would bring them to the stand at the Fair. Everything was 10 cents those first years — ice cream sandwiches, nutsticks, and popsicles.

Don made the nutsticks from pints of ice cream, cutting them in triangles and dipping them in chocolate, which came in half-gallon jars. Each year, the nutsticks became more popular, and the size of the chocolate containers went to gallon cans and then to five-gallon pails. The ice cream for cutting the nutsticks went from pints to quarts and then to half-gallons.

Eventually, we tried to make them starting a week before the Fair. Storage space was a problem, but neighbors helped by offering space in their freezers. One day, one of our neighbors came to us with a large handful of sticks. She said, "I guess I owe you for all these nutsticks — the babysitter and the kids sampled them, really liked them, and ate lots!" We just laughed and said we were glad they didn't get sick from eating so many.

For 25 years, from 1948 until 1972 — except for one year when Don was in Korea — having the stand at the Fair was a regular part of summer for us. Don's sisters, Anne and Shirley, helped us, and as our kids got old enough, they helped, too.

When we raised the price from 10 cents to 15 cents, no one complained. But when we raised the price to 25 cents, we heard some say, "Boy, I'm not going to pay that much!" Eventually they'd come back and get some anyway.

In 1972, when we decided it would be our last year, we never dreamed how often someone would mention the Fair and the nutsticks. Even now, when Fair time is here, someone will say, "Nutsticks were a part of the Fair for us."

How different it is now, seeing all the neat trailers of the food vendors at the Fair. But one thing that never changes is how much everyone loves the Great Jones County Fair.

Don and Irma Skelley
Monticello

Don Skelley at the famous nutstick stand in 1950.

A Copper Kettle, a Table, a Candy Hook

For more than 100 years, the Jones County Fair was famous for its cream candy. During all of that time, it was made by only two men: the legendary "Candy Bill" Leech, who moved with the Fair from Anamosa to Monticello in 1874, and Cecil Farmer, who made the taffy from 1930 until his death in 1975.

Cecil Farmer's daughter, Janet Nesley, says her father learned how to make the candy from Candy Bill. "He made the candy day and night," she says. "He started long before the Fair and packed the bars in boxes. Everyone loved it. We had lemon, black walnut, chocolate, strawberry and vanilla flavors. The black walnuts came from our own tree, in our yard at 107 South Sales Street in Anamosa."

In his screened stand at the Fair, Farmer had a copper kettle, a cooling table, and a candy hook on the wall (Candy Bill had fastened his candy hook to a big maple tree).

"I remember that Dad seemed to be doing a kind of dance, pulling the candy out and slapping it back on the hook," Janet says. He spread the warm taffy out on the table, shaped it into bars, and she and her mother wrapped each individually. "Lots of people from Cedar Rapids would come and buy dozens," she remembers.

A special treat, handed to youngsters out the back door, was the "hot snitch," a piece of warm candy left over when the taffy was made into bars.

Even now, the Fair is an important part of summer for Janet, her children and grandchildren. "We have so many memories," she says. "We still go to the Fair every year."

Shade trees help Fairgoers cool off.

Community participation keeps breaking records. In 2001, there were 1,500 entries in Open Exhibits. The average number of entries in 4H-FFA classes is nearly 1,800.

Then there are the thousands who support the Fair just by being there — year after year. They look forward to seeing old friends who also come every year, and they're missed if they miss a day.

"You always see people you've known from years back," says Bob Nowachek of Wyoming. "There's always somebody who comes up to you. A year ago, we had hay down and I stayed home. It was the first fair I'd missed since 1937. They said, 'Where's Bob Nowachek? He's always here!'"

More than 100 years ago, the editor of the

The airplane was a novelty at the 1915 Fair.

Monticello Express wrote: "In good weather and amid showers and passing rain, in sunshine and in storm, the fair has been held each year developing some excellence over the ones preceding. The little saplings set out here became beautiful shade trees, furnishing shade and shelter for all on the grounds. The young men and maidens who in early years of the Fair did their courting on the fairgrounds are now middle aged and married people and they will not fail to take their children to the beautiful spot where they loved wisely and well."

Tradition and nostalgia claim the hearts of all fair-goers. Beautiful grounds and a remarkable sense of community account for much of that certain "some-thing" about the Great Jones County Fair. But there are people who say there's still more: the willingness to change with the times.

Through the years, the Fair had added new attractions each year, introducing modern inventions and entertainments as they came into being — from Edison's phonograph to bungee jumping. When electricity came to the Fairgrounds in 1915, a new era of nighttime shows and carnivals began. Radio personalities started to make appearances. By the 1950s, the "Big Bands" were drawing crowds to the grandstand. Television and recording artists appeared regularly on the county-fair circuit.

Then something happened that created a new picture. Varlyn recalls: "About 1970, the whole concept of entertainment was changing. There were auditorium

Big stunts and big-name acts draw people to the Fair.

shows at the Five Seasons Center in Cedar Rapids, Hawkeye athletics…people had more money and could afford to take a bigger trip, to the State Fair or out-of-state."

In the early 1980s, falling attendance prompted the Fair board to take a closer look at what was happening. One rainy night, there were fewer than 300 people in the audience. Joe Legg, retired county extension director, remembers. "Everyone took a new look at the Fair," he says. "I was on that board, and I saw it happen."

With a renewed openness to change, the Fair has since achieved a reputation for first-rate attractions.

Many recent performers have been CMA and ACM award winners. "Now you have a rainy night, and you still have thousands of people there," says Varlyn.

So that elusive "something about the Jones County Fair" has been defined in these three ways — but is there more? Is there still an indefinable mystique? Maybe so. Listen to county extension director Joe Yedlik: "When I talk with extension directors in other counties, they tell me, 'My job would be great if it wasn't for the fair.' It's totally different for me. It's more than just a job. It's more than just a Fair."

Joe is right. It's the Great Jones County Fair — the Five Best Days of Summer.

THE 124th GREAT JONES COUNTY FAIR

AUGUST 11 - 15, 1976
MONTICELLO, IOWA

Ten Flavors, Seven Ounces, One Nickel

The week of the Great Jones County Fair was a summer high point for my family and me. My stepfather, Glenn Bancroft, owned and operated the Monticello Bottling Works. He was the sole supplier of the soft drinks sold at the Fair during the 1930s and early 1940s.

The Monticello Bottling Works was located on Second Street. Glenn and his father, Hiram, had bought the business from Cecil Curtis in the 1920s. After his father died, Glenn continued to put out the pop with the help of one employee, Clarence Eggers, my three sisters, my brother David and me.

We all washed bottles. I started when I was 10. It was a no-fun kids' job, which we did two or three times a week. First the bottles were put into the washer, a big tank containing sanitizing solution, then into a rinsing tank. The bottles were then taken out two by two and put on a brushing device to clean them inside and out. After they were rinsed again and inspected for flaws, they were put into pop cases to be filled.

Glenn mixed the pop, pouring a 100-pound bag of sugar into 49 gallons of water to make the syrup, and then adding the flavoring extracts. One bottle at a time, the bottles were filled with this mixture, carbonated water at 60 pounds of pressure was added, and the bottles were capped.

This made a drink with lots of fizz — lemon, orange, strawberry, root beer, cream soda, blood orange, lime rickey, orange pineapple, gingerale and grape. A seven-ounce bottle sold for a nickel.

Producing 80 cases of pop took five hours, but you had to hustle — and we did. Glenn Bancroft taught me how to work, and I appreciate that now.

We supplied pop to cafes, taverns and grocery stores in Monticello, Prairieburg, Delhi, Hopkinton, Center Junction, Scotch Grove, Langworthy, Onslow, Cascade, Wyoming and Oxford Junction. Cascade drank more pop per capita than any of the other stops.

Summer was our busiest season, and Fair week really tried all our resources. We used all available bottles and made pop every day to supply the Fair and our regular customers, too.

The larger, modern mechanized companies eventually drove the smaller bottling works out of business, but I still have people telling me how good that Bancroft pop tasted at the Great Jones County Fair.

Wesley G. "Bud" Hanken
Monticello

"When you grew up on a farm in Jones County,
there were two things you knew you were going to do.
One was go to church, and the other was join 4-H."

FAMILIES, FRIENDS AND FUN

John Harms has known the Nowacheks and the Brunscheens for a long time, and when he makes that statement they laugh and nod in agreement.

"I wouldn't trade those days for anything," says Shirlee Brunscheen. "Other people used to wonder how we knew so many kids. It was through 4-H."

The Nowacheks and the Brunscheens are three-generation 4-H families, and the two families have been friends for all of those years. The grandfathers — good friends Robert Nowachek and Donald Brunscheen — competed against each other in live-stock compe-titions more than 60 years ago.

"I had the grand champion steer in 1941," Bob said. "Donnie had the reserve champion.

But I never mentioned to him that I beat him."

Bob joined 4-H in 1938, when he was 16. "I was always interested in it," he says. "My uncle had black cattle, and one day he said 'Why don't you have a calf?' We picked out a calf. Then I got two other calves. We had the champion pen-of-three that year."

Bob's son Ron was a 4-H member from 1962 to 1971. He, too, showed champions — the champion heifer in 1968 and the reserve champion in 1970. John has fun needling Ron: "The first year of the commercial heifer class, I got first and Ron got second," he says. Camaraderie is typical of 4-H. "It's a grass roots kind of thing," Ron says. "You get involved in more things through the years, outside your own family niche." Ron, Eugene Brunscheen and

(Continued on page 25)

JONES
COUNTY FAIR
MONTICELLO, IOWA, 1941
Boys & Girls Club Exhibitor
I'm
of

Robert Nowachek and his 1941 champion steer.

Celebrating 100 Years of 4-H

The 150th Great Jones County Fair is one of the officially designated sites in Iowa for the observance this summer of the 100th anniversary of 4-H.

Organized nationally in 1902 with the goal of providing better agricultural education to young people, 4-H continues to emphasize "learning by doing." Most states, including Iowa, organized clubs with rural parents acting as volunteer leaders, and county extension agents providing materials.

Through the years, the 4-H objective has remained the same: the development of youth as individuals and as responsible and productive citizens.

Although individual projects were carried out earlier, the first Jones County 4-H clubs were organized in 1925. John Wilcox, president of the Dairy Calf Club, was awarded a trip to the 4-H Club Congress and International Livestock Show as the "most worthy club member in the county." Fannie Mae Hicks's calf won first place in the 1926 Baby Beef Club. There were six girls' clubs with 75 members. (Girls could have livestock projects, but they were required to complete home economics projects, as well.)

Wilma Merfeld remembers the annual 4-H Rally Days. When Wilma was a 4-H member, in the 1930s, a 4-H queen was elected each year and crowned as part of the Rally Day program. Hundreds of girls and their leaders attended. A newspaper account of the 1932 meeting told of the crowning of Florence Mardorf:

"Following a picnic dinner which was served at noon, a George and Martha Washington pageant

"I pledge my Head to clearer thinking, my Heart to greater loyalty, my Hands to larger service, and my Health to better living…for my Club, my community, my country and my world."

was presented. Florence Mardorf of the Wise Owl Club of Jackson Township was queen of the 4-H girls of Jones County. Other candidates acted as her attendants. They formed an archway through which three little girls, Alice Clark, Eileen Loomis and Ruth Ann Hintz, preceded the procession.

"They were followed by the queen, who was welcomed by George and Martha Washington, played by Mrs. E.C. Gotsch and Mrs. B.D. Heiken. George placed a crown of roses on the head of the queen and the 'Ceremonial Song' was sung by Edna Schoon."

The Great Jones County Fair has served as the showcase for 4-H achievements. In 1961, the new Youth Center building at the Fair, though not quite completed, was used for the first time. "Along with the added space," wrote 4-H club historian Dorothy Freese, " a demonstration room was initiated. To many who had once demonstrated in a tent, they realized this was a blessing."

There were 679 4-H members in 40 clubs that year. The girls exhibited more than 1,350 items of clothing. Boys' projects included beef cattle (349 enrolled); 20 pens of junior feeders; dairy heifers (185 enrolled); swine (100); sheep (16); and a new horse-and-pony project (20). Seventeen boys participated in a five-acre corn project.

Only one change has been made in the 4-H pledge since its official adoption in 1927. In 1973, it was revised to include "and my world."

Shirlee Jansen were all part of a larger group of 4-H friends who grew up together. No one was surprised that Gene and Shirlee later married.

While Ron and Gene showed heifers and steers, Shirlee showed mainly steers. "My folks didn't have a cow-calf herd. They would feed out cattle, so I showed steers. It was exciting to be in the livestock parade at the Fair. At night, before the entertainment started, you'd walk your animal from the barn, up the track. You'd give your name to the announcer and parade in front of the crowd in the stands. The champions would get their trophies right there, in front of the crowd."

John remembers that it was "the time of night when cattle are friskiest. We'd often come back on a dead run. Some would get loose. It was actually dangerous — we'd have 300 head out there." In those days, of course, there weren't 2,200 people sitting in folding chairs on the track.

"I never liked selling my steer," Shirlee says. "When you took your steer up for the auction, you left it and walked on up the hill. Then you had to be careful not to come back while it was still there. It was easier if it was gone when you came back down. I always said that if I had children, they would show heifers — we could keep them and put them in the herd."

When Shirlee was raising livestock as her 4-H projects, she was required to fulfill all of the girls' 4-H requirements as well. This meant cooking and sewing,

Gene Brunsheen with his 1967 champion heifer.

Shirlee Jansen with her champion Shorthorn, 1967.

The Ron Nowachek family takes a break during the '92 Fair.

making presentations, giving demonstrations. And with everything, the time-honored 4-H process of setting goals at the beginning of the year and keeping careful records. "It was a challenge," she says. "All those projects and doing beef…two clubs, two books to keep. But I loved the livestock part of it." She once won her class (out of 74 head) at the International Livestock Show in Chicago.

Gene and Shirlee's daughters, Lisa, 26, and Kris, 22, have also been 4-H members. "I wanted to get Lisa involved in showing cattle," Shirlee says, "so we contacted John and bought a heifer from him. That heifer is still in our herd, and has twins about every other year."

John says, "Shirlee and the girls have these heifers they've raised and shown, and they're all in the herd, being productive. But if you walk out in the pasture, they'll come over and lick you!"

Like their parents, Lisa and Kris have more trophies and plaques than they have space for. They have shown champions in many heifer classes, and they've had a lot of support from their parents. "The more hair you can get on an animal, the better you can get it to look," Shirlee says. "We have an insulated building with a two-ton air conditioner, to help grow hair during the summer."

Ron and Carmen Nowachek's daughters are Dena, 25, Katie, 22, and Lori, 18. All three girls have shown champion steers, and they've earned many rate-of-gain awards. In her last year in 4-H, Dena's steer was the

(Continued on page 30)

The signature uniform of 4-H girls

Sewing projects were a big part of girls' 4-H activities.

WISE CLUB Jackson Twp.

Quick Tricks Make Slick Chicks

The Great Jones County Fair holds many fond memories for me. I was a 4-H member for eight years, with my most active years being from 1952-56 when I was in high school. The summers were spent working on 4-H projects, whether it was picking out the best vegetables for a garden box, sewing a dress or sanding a bedside table. Then there was a demonstration (now called a presentation) to prepare for, with catchy titles such as "Quick Tricks Make Slick Chicks" or "Cool, Crisp, and Crammed with Vitamins."

Carol Benhart Hall Brinkman and I did a special demonstration one year of "Making Kolaches." We considered this a tribute to our moms for the active part they also had taken in 4-H. But it was not all work. Many fun hours were spent going on rides, eating a nut bar and strolling the Midway, keeping an eye out for that "special guy." The Fair was a wonderful way to end a busy summer. I know 4-H has changed a lot, but I hope 4-Hers today experience the work, fun and thrill of learning that we did almost 50 years ago.

Judy Ingwersen Cannon
Pensacola, Florida

Donald Brunsheen and his 1240-pound reserve champion Hereford, 1941.

When Black Angus Were New

Livestock exhibits at the earliest fairs in Jones County included cows, horses, sheep and hogs. One of the first awards made was a cash prize of $10 to J.M. Peet for "the best cultivated farm." Other exhibits included apples, cheese, grapes and homemade cloth.

Gail McNeill writes in "Monticello, 1836-1986" that the horse show in 1889 included Percherons, Percheron-Normans and Clydesdales. "Special attention was also given to a herd of Black Aberdeen Angus owned by W.S. Niles of Wyoming. It was evidently an unfamiliar breed in this locality, for the local newspaper predicted, 'These glossy, hornless cattle will rapidly gain in favor.'"

By 1925, corn was the main crop in Jones County. It had become a livestock region, with practically all of the grain (corn, oats and barley) and hay consumed within the county. Dairy predominated in the northern townships. Hybrid corn, entirely new to many people, was displayed at the Farm Bureau booth in 1932.

Beef entries grew tremendously through the 1930s. In 1936, 55 calves were exhibited by 33 boys. The 1937 baby beef show was notable for the grand champion Shorthorn shown by George Fraser. It won another grand championship at the Iowa State Fair, then went on to win first place in the Shorthorn division at the International Livestock Exposition in Chicago.

In 1944, the innovative "Fat Steer Show" was held for the first time, attracting national attention and entries from all over the country.

Brainchild of H.M. Carpenter, Jr., the Fat Steer Show was judged by packinghouse buyers. Awards were based solely on market values, not show ring points. By 1949, it was ranked as one of the nation's four top shows, and drew entries and spectators from other states. Now called the "Prime Steer Show," it remains one of the most popular agricultural events at the Fair.

FIRST PREMIUM

GREAT JONES COUNTY FAIR

MONTICELLO, IOWA

1941

SECOND PREMIUM

AT JONES UNTY AIR

ELLO, IOWA 941

champion. Ron remembers that Lori had a black steer that got reserve champion in 1993, and Katie had a red steer that won. And some day, Dena's two children may be taking home trophies as the fourth 4-H generation in the family.

"Our daughters did the girls' side of it, too," Ron says. "I think it was a good learning experience for them. I know they hated to do the record books, and the presentations — they'd say, 'Why do I have to do this!' But when they look back, they appreciate it.

"The kids would show their livestock projects, then we would take the steers and later we'd put them in the prime steer show. I was lucky enough to win that one year." Therein lies a story: Ron celebrated with friends in the beer tent. "I came over early the next morning," his dad says with a grin, "and the cattle were out. They were all over the place, and Ronnie was out there with a hangover, trying to round them up. He was having a heck of a time!" Ron's friends haven't let him forget.

The Nowacheks and the Brunscheens are typical of the many 4-H families in Jones County. There are trophies, ribbons and plaques from three generations, and books full of carefully kept records and pictures.

Looking at them, you might think that nothing has changed over the years. You would be wrong.

Shirlee points to a photograph in one of her books: "Cattle were so short," she says, "and we used to put a lot of straw under them to make their legs look shorter for the picture. Sometimes they looked like they didn't have any legs at all. Nowadays, cattle are so big — when our girls were younger, we could hardly get them in the picture."

Bob Nowachek says, "There's a big difference in cattle today. Cross breeding has given us a lot of exotics. It's made a lot more tonnage of meat."

In a broader sense, farming and 4-H have both gone through tremendous periods of change. Joe Yedlik, county extension education director, and his predecessor, Joe Legg, now retired, say there are not only fewer 4-H members, but fewer farms than there were 40 years ago. In the 1950s, Joe Legg recalls, "4-H was really strong. Jones County had the second-highest membership in the state. We had to restrict livestock entries, had to tell kids 'Two calves is all you can show.'"

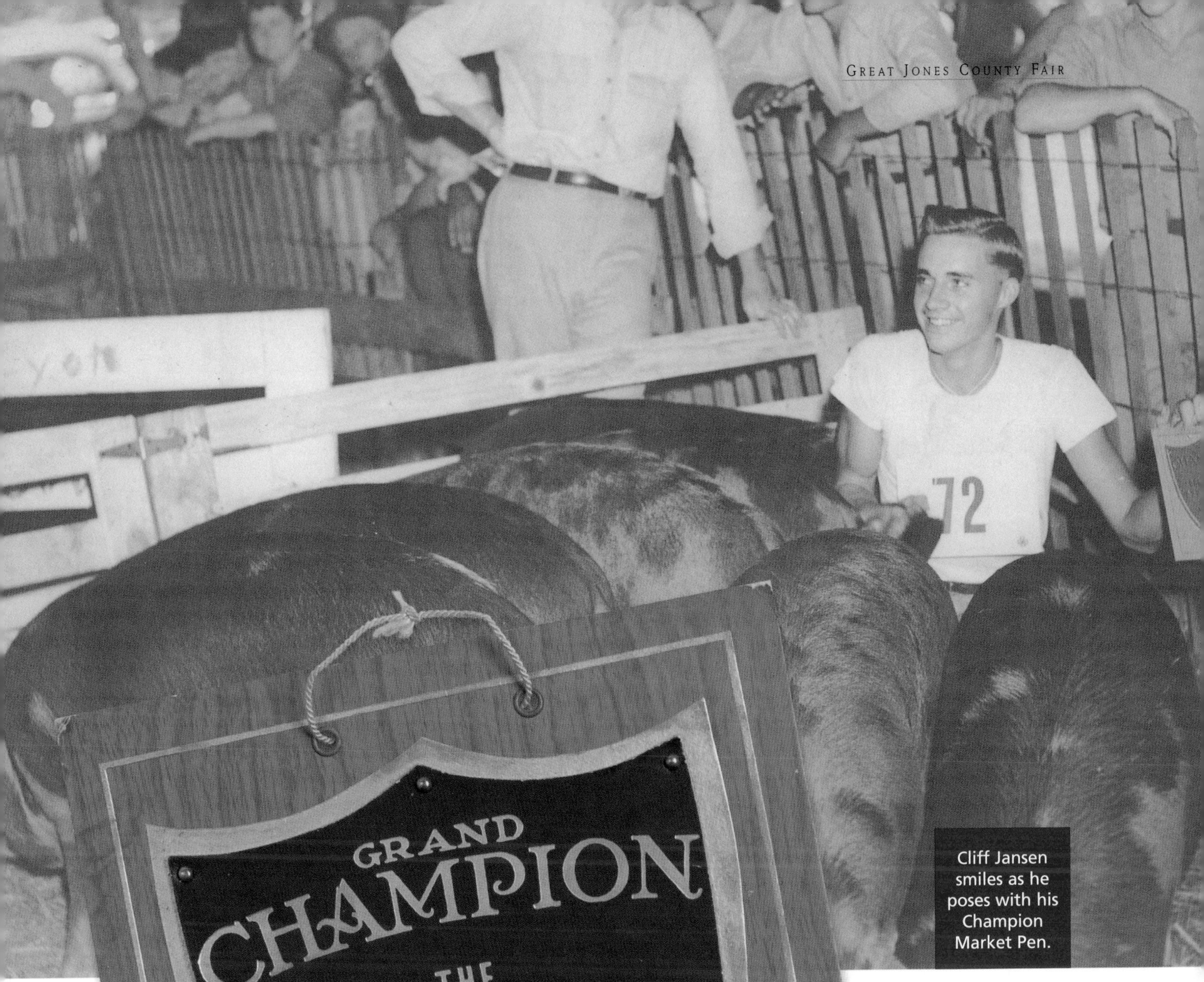

GRAND CHAMPION

THE GREAT JONES COUNTY FAIR

MONTICELLO, IA. 1946

Cliff Jansen smiles as he poses with his Champion Market Pen.

This must be where the phrase "Hog Heaven" originated!

4-H boys in line to get exhibition numbers.

A textile/clothing demonstration circa 1930.

Demonstrations are a big part of the 4-H experience.

Winners come in all shapes, sizes and ages!

Varlyn Fink, who was 4-H youth director in those days, notes that young people started leaving the farms to live elsewhere during the past 30 or 40 years. "Today, there are fewer farms and fewer farms with livestock," he says.

Today, says Joe Yedlik, "4-H membership is half of what it used to be. The difference is the population of the county. So 4-H has added other types of projects — woodworking projects and small animals, for example.

"It's also true that there's so much for youngsters to do these days — they have so many choices as they get older, with school activities and jobs. What we're seeing now in 4-H is a great influx of young members, fifth graders." A new class is the "fastest-growing livestock" project — a calf born during the Fair year. "It's a small animal that kids can handle," Joe says. "Boys and girls of all ages can get started this way. They'll keep records, talk to the judge about their calf, and show it at the Fair."

Varlyn says 4-H continues to be one of the most stable parts of the Fair, even though its membership is smaller. "Today, it's not uncommon for a youngster to bring five to seven projects, all in different areas."

"The Fair has really grown," says Joe Legg. "We started with tents…we used to put them on the slope. Below that was another tent, where we put the sheep. One night it rained so hard…

A Ribbon Winner from Japan

In 1980, we hosted Tetzu Shimizu from Tokyo as part of the Jones County 4-H LABO Program Exchange. Tetzu, Jerry and Terry Sorgenfrey became best buddies. Tetzu told his parents, "Sorgenfreys so rich, so big farm." I explained that we weren't rich, but all farmers needed that much room to farm.

The next summer, Tetzu's sister, Ai, came to stay with us. She was only 11, and was extremely homesick. Since she had brought origami supplies with her, I encouraged her to make an origami hanging mobile. She did, and entered it in the open art class at the Jones County Fair. She won a purple ribbon and several blue ribbons on other origami items.

Pat Sorgenfrey
Onslow

4-H Rewards Four Generations

We are four generations of 4-H members who have participated in Jones County Fair events. Grandpa Henry Tobiason and his family were avid Fairgoers. I remember that one year he raised seven of the 10 winners in the Fat Steer Show. Uncle George Tobiason was a 4-H member, too, and showed many winning Angus cattle. Dad (Richard Antons) was a 4-H leader for the Center Junction Royal Rustlers 4-H Club. Sister Karen and I are nine-year members. Now our children, Christine, Charlie and Sarah, are active members.

As a girl, I was required to join both the South Sunshine Girls and Center Junction Royal Rustlers 4-H clubs in order to exhibit livestock. At first I was the only girl in the boys' club. It was fun raising and showing the baby beeves and horses, but I also did two record books and presentations for two clubs — I thought it was discrimination!

We also had to sew our girls' uniform. It was a green pin-striped blouse and skirt. I remember that this was not my favorite activity.

I vividly recall my first and favorite baby beef. We called him Andy. He was so tame Karen could ride him. She rode Andy up the hill to the sale ring under the trees north of the exhibit hall now known as the Berndes Center.

Another highlight of my 4-H years was passing out ribbons at the Fair as Hereford Queen and, the next year, as Jones County Beef Princess.

For my family and me, our 4-H experiences are some of the most educational, exciting and rewarding times of our lives.

Sharon Antons Roller
Monticello

Jean Brodersen is all smiles as 4-H Queen in 1933.

Dixie Hanken and "Angel," her champion Holstein, circa 1953.

those sheep were really wet."

Back in those days, there was a dormitory up near the show ring. John says, "Traveling wasn't as easy back then. The dorm had bunks and cots, and you paid a buck and a half to stay in it. It was supervised, but some real liability issues surfaced in the 1970s, taking care of the kids, so it was given up." For Shirlee, nothing was lost: "The guys could stay in the dorm, but the girls had to go home," she says.

Scoring the competitions doesn't cause as many late nights as it used to. Computers have taken over much of the calculation. But Joe Yedlik still brings his camper and stays at the Fair overnight. He used to do it because of the late nights and the need to be ready for the next day. "Then," he says, "when we started using computers, we needed a place to put them. We found that an air-conditioned camper was a lot nicer and kept the computers cleaner."

With or without computers, Joe would still camp at the Fair overnight. "That's the way I was raised," he says, "staying overnight at the Fair in a truck with a tarp over it, on a cot. One of my earliest memories is leading my cow into the show ring. When I go to the Fair, I want to be part of it."

Joe's feelings about the Fair are shared by Varlyn, who remembers: "Back in the '60s we used to have the hog show on Monday before the Fair opened. My wife went into labor during the hog show, so I went back to Anamosa. After our daughter Chris was born, I went back to the hog show. It was August 18th."

John, who has moved on from farming to a number of other business interests — and who also serves as Fair manager — is as enthusiastic about his 4-H background as he is about the Fair. "4-H is a way of life for rural families," he says. "The Fair is the showcase. When it comes time to get livestock ready at Fair time, it's family members who do the grooming, not hired professionals. The whole family is involved in the project.

"The basis of any fair is agriculture. Agriculture originated the "family, friends and fun" atmosphere of the Fair. And the agricultural economy has a great influence on the Fair. When there's a good growing season, it's a good Fair."

Go to the Fair!

More than 100 years ago, a newspaper writer gave a dozen reasons to attend the Jones County Fair:

"Go to the Fair — because you want a week of respite from your farm, because you want to see your neighbor and compare notes — the best method of education; because you want to see the best horses, cattle, sheep, and swine and compare their merits; because you desire to see fruits and flowers and products of art, these rich and helpful and beautiful results of our highest civilization and best culture.

"Go because you want your boys to rub up against the world and not get rubbed out; go because you want your girls to know better than to walk hand in hand with a greenhorn, sucking a stick of candy and laughing like a squealing calf, and because you'd have them acquire tastes, ideas, and habits corresponding to intelligence and refinement of the age in which they live.

"Go to compare yourself, your family and your products with your neighbors. After the comparison many an animal gets better care, many a farm looks neater, and a brighter touch comes to many a home also."

Ken Streeper shows his champion Brown Swiss in 1946.

Ken's grandson, Nicholas Hein, carries on the tradition 50 years later.

Friends, families and spectators watch as judges go to work in 1933.

Flowers, from asters to zinnias. Stock cars. Lemonade. Harness racing. Tilt-a-whirl. Sand sculpture. Hot dogs. Baseball. Beer. Ferris wheel. Heifers and hogs, and an artist who makes woodcarvings with a chain saw.

SOMETHING FOR EVERYONE

What's your pleasure? You can have it your way at the Great Jones County Fair.

"When I was a kid," says Allen Westhoff, "I lived down the street from the Fairgrounds. I used to go there and watch Carl Hein, Tom Eden, Pete Miller — all those guys — training their horses. Brad Ashby was around here a lot, too. I guess I was 15 or 16 years old. I really liked working with horses. I was about 21 when I became 'superintendent of speed.' Was I qualified? Probably not."

Al must have known enough to do a good job; he was in charge of the harness races for years. He served on the Fair board, and was Fair manager from 1983 to 1989. Today, he manages the Josephine County Fair in Grants Pass, Oregon. He loves fairs, and he loves horses.

Harness racing has been a part of the Great Jones County Fair since its beginning, with the first recorded racing purse won in 1865 by a horse named "Buckskin." Interest in racing dropped off a little in the early 1900s, but came back strongly during the 1940s.

It was about this time that Carl Hein got into harness racing. He and his wife farmed near Monticello, raising three sons — Dale, Glen and Melvin. Dale remembers that "the Jones County Fair was always a big thing with my dad. There was no excuse for not being at the Fair. My mother would fix chicken and we'd take a lunch. It was a big day."

When Carl Hein started harness racing, Dale says, "My mother couldn't understand it. She thought we were going to the poor farm because he wasn't spending enough time taking care of things at home. But later on, she got so she enjoyed it, too."

The names of Carl Hein and Tom Eden became legendary among Fair racing fans. They

A trotter moves the front leg on one side with the back leg on the other side.

Harness
racing at
the Fair
in 1950

were the horsemen Al Westhoff had idolized as a kid, when they were training their horses at the Jones County Fairgrounds. Both men suffered tremendous losses when the Fair horse barn burned in December of 1960.

Tammy Eden Huie says 20 horses died, and her father lost eight trotters and pacers. The total loss, she recalls, was more than $50,000.

"I'd never seen my dad so down," Dale says. "He lost four head in the fire, and he said he wasn't going to start over — he was too old. Tom Eden lost a very good horse in that fire."

Encouraged by his sons, Carl finally did buy a new horse — named Gene C. — which won the first Hawkeye Colt Stakes. Carl wanted Dale to start racing, but Dale, a veterinarian, didn't feel he had the time.

Nevertheless, he applied for a license to drive harness races.

"We went to watch Dad race one time, but he was having trouble breathing and told me to drive the colt. So that's how I started driving. Then Dad died and left the horses to me, and that settled that. I have a friend who worried about me that first year. He said he was afraid I'd get 'dust-a-monia,' I was so far back."

As a new driver, Dale felt even more keenly the typical race-day excitement. An old-timer told him, "You're going to be nervous, and the horse is going to know that. They pick it up through the reins. The thing to do is pretend you're not nervous. Don't let 'em know."

A driver for more than 30 years, Dale is now one of the senior members of the racing fraternity. Recently

census showed 2,011 farms in county in 1959. This com- with 2,080 farms reported in county and the 1,961 farms

per cent of its operators owned the land they worked and Fayette county noted 63.1 percent were owners - operators.

OAT CROP COMPARED
Jones county's average oat yield per acre was 44.5 bushels while Cedar reported 51.2 and Jackson's was 41.0.

the lowest, with the Jackson, in Jones county wh ported 2,108 acres.
Cedar reported 5,453, J

THURSDAY
DECEMBER 29, 1960
MONTICELLO, IOWA
Volume 95
Number 72

The Monticello E
One of America's Greatest Weekl

$50,000 Fire Destroys Barn; 20 Valuable Hor

Five Civil Cases Are Filed; Rule Mistrial

Five new cases were filed last week in Jones county district court Judge B. J. M. Maxwell ruled a mistrial in another civil case.

One case, filed Dec. 24, was settled out of court Tuesday morning. The Citizens Savings Bank of Anamosa filed suit last Saturday against William J. Jansen, Monticello, in which the plaintiff sought payment on a promissory note issued July 12, 1960. The plaintiff had asked for $121.20 with interest at the rate of seven percent after Sept. 12, 1960, plus costs.

DIVORCE SUITS FILED
Two suits for divorce were filed Friday, Dec. 23. Phyllis King, Jones county, asks for a divorce from Warren T. King of Wisconsin. The plaintiff also seeks the care and custody of two minor children, reasonable child support, any further equitable release as may seem just and proper, attorney fees and costs.

According to the petition, the couple was married Oct. 17, 1954 at Kehoka, Mo., and separated

Nov. 26, 1956. The plaintiff charges desertion.

On the same day, Jean Augustus, Jones county, filed suit for divorce from Keith Augustus. According to the petition, they were married Mar. 16, 1958 at Council Bluffs and lived together until September, 1960. There are two minor children.

The plaintiff charges cruel and inhuman treatment. She asks for the divorce, custody of the children, permanent child support, for the property of the parties, that the defendant pay debts of the parties,

(Cont'd on page A-4)

Hearings on Railroad Cuts Jan. 24, 25

Hearings on proposals to reduce railroad freight service affecting two Jones county areas will be held next month, the State Commission announced this week.

The hearings are:
Jan. 24 at Independ waukee Road propos

Twenty horses were burned to death early last Thursday morning when a large barn at the fairgrounds in Monticello was destroyed by fire. Loss of the horses, building and equipment exceeded $50,000.

Defective wiring may have caused the blaze, authorities said. Frank Barnts, who discovered the fire, said the blaze started near a water pump in the barn.

Barnts discovered the fire shortly before 6:30 a.m. when he went to the barn to care for a horse belonging to Dean Tedrow. Barnts attempted to put out the blaze with a sack, but it was already out of control. A wooden box around the base of the pump was burned out, Barnts said, and the fire spread quickly to nearby stalls.

Barnts led the Tedrow horse to safety and then attempted to return for the other horses but was driven back by the smoke and flames. He then ran to the street, stopped a passing car and asked the driver to call the Monticello fire department.

The fire had broken through the roof of the structure by the time help arrived. Firemen battled the blaze in the sub-zero weather but were unable to save the building.

Barnts said he believed many of the horses were already overcome by smoke when he arrived at the barn because they were not making any noise. The Tedrow horse was humped in a corner and was groggy from the smoke, he said.

Sixteen of the horses lost in the blaze were harness horses. Loss of

Specht Family Inj In Traffic Accide

Three Monticello resid among four persons injure car crash on highway 1 Manchester late Monday.

Max Specht, 46, Montice of one of the cars, receive Cyril Gavin, 45, Ryan, shoulder injury.

Mrs. Specht, a passen husband's car, suffered chest and their daughter, 15, suffered a broken arr

Named Cham Corn Grower

M. P. Paulsen of Cent has been named area cha grower in the Eastern cluding 19 counties, it wa by Farmers Hybrid Seed pany of Hampton, spon contest.

Paulsen's record sh plication of sound land practices and the use of brid varieties. His rec bushels per acre was "Farmers" No. 322. T adjusted to a uniform b percent moisture. T is the yield of No. 2 co

A personalized, eng was awarded to Paul an annual award pre Farmers Hybrid Seed to those who produce

Opening Bookkeeping and Tax Service Here

The Fair experiences its greatest tragedy in 1960.

his horse lost its head number as they came out onto the track. "I usually got off the cart and picked it up when this happened," Dale said, "but I had seen all the younger guys just reach down and swipe the number, so I tried to do the same. I fell off the cart. After the race, a guy came up to me and said, 'Hey Doc, we're looking for free acts for our fair in Eldon. Would you be interested?'"

Dale and his wife, Althea, who is also a native of Monticello, live in Elkader and spend most of the summer on the harness racing circuit. They still have one brood mare, Patsy Cooper, that traces back to his dad's Patsy Moka.

Another kind of racing means "having it your way" to John Myers. Stock cars are his favorite event. When he was in high school, John says, "Dick White and I would sit in the box seats for the stock car races. We'd sit on two of the folding chairs and hold the other two chairs in front of us to block the mud that was flying up from the track.

"The old grandstand had a canvas roof," John says, "and every time it rained, the canvas would collect water. Then, when it got heavy enough, the water would suddenly fall off.

"I remember one year when I was old enough to drive, Grandma rented a parking spot for me right

(Continued on page 46)

Carl Hein cruises along behind his trotter, Patsy Hardy.

See How They Run

Are trotters born or made? Both, says Dale Hein, who has been racing trotters for more than 30 years. "It's in the blood lines," he says, "but training is also important. We use weights on their toes and different shoes. These horses are a thing of beauty if they're just right. It's like ballet."

Only about 20 percent of the harness horses in the United States are trotters; the others are pacers. A trotter moves the front leg on one side of its body and the hind leg on the other side at the same time. A pacer moves the legs on the same side of its body together.

Pacers are more dangerous than trotters, Dale says. "They wear hobbles to keep them in stride. Until they get used to them, they can stumble and fall. The next horse can get through the wreckage, but the cart can't, and the driver can be thrown 30 or 40 feet in the air.

"Trotters don't fall easily, because if they break stride they can gallop out of the way. They're a little harder to drive because they don't have the hobbles — there's so much in the lines. You've got to think like the horse, feel when he's going to do something and help him. You've got to stay focused."

near the main gate. It rained so hard that the races were delayed. Then they called on the audience to come out and drive their cars around to help pack down the track. You had to go the opposite of the way the stock cars normally do. So I went out and got my car, and I did that. Was that a muddy mess!"

Carol Myers is also a stock car fan. "My folks always went to the Fair for the stock car races on Saturday," she says. " We would pack chicken and potato salad, and sit on the hill. We went home when the races were over. But when John and I got married, we started going every year for the whole week."

The passion for cars runs in the family. Their daughter Jenny, who has been to every Fair since she was six months old, also has a favorite event: the stock car races. (Or is it the demolition derby? Jenny has trouble deciding.)

First introduced at the Fair in 1950, the stock car races made a big hit. They drew 25,000 spectators that year, and haven't lost their popularity since. They are an example of the Fair board's efforts through the years to keep up with the times — to bring new and different events, to introduce new inventions and to demonstrate the newest national fad.

In the late 1800s there were bands of Indians, hot air balloon ascensions, herds of antelope and buffalo, bicycle races, an exhibition of the new college game of football, and Edison's phonograph — the marvelous "talking machine."

In 1899, the first catcher's mask came to baseball, introduced at the Fair by H.M. Carpenter, Sr.,

(Continued on page 50)

Merrill and Larry Hughes prerace 1965.

Gus Hughes and his parents after a 1996 feature win.

Jay Iben battles for the lead in a 1978 feature.

The Hughes brothers show off their hardware in 1997.

Tom Hughes takes a victory lap in 1963.

Feature winner Ron Barker with his crew in 2000.

The Best 4½ Days of Summer

"Good weather for lemonade stands but hard on stand-up collars." That was the way it was in 1900, when stifling heat kept Fairgoers away.

Weather has always had an impact on the Fair. Some years have been especially memorable. Consider, for example, the 1983 Fair, when 100-degree temperatures and high humidity prevailed. Or 1985, when a heat wave was broken by a three-inch downpour and heavy lightening, which put an end to the Thursday night show.

Or 1993, one of the wettest Iowa summers on record. Flooding and heavy rains washed away many of the 10,000 parking spaces at the Monticello Golf Club. The Fair board hastily arranged for parking on streets, at schools and at private businesses, and ran shuttle buses to the Fairground. Workers had to pump standing water from the track, and fill in mud holes with rock.

The Fair was favored with sunshine until Saturday, when rain washed out the afternoon events — causing manager Andy Anderson to call it "the best four-and-a-half days of summer."

Lofty Competition at Anamosa

During the years when the Anamosa fair competed with the Great Jones County Fair, Anamosa always tried to be first with sensational acts. In 1913, the Anamosa people decided they wanted a parachute drop from an airplane. They sent a committee to Chicago to see Max Lillie, a daredevil flyer. Lillie was concerned that if a man jumped from the plane, the shift in weight might cause the plane to crash. The story is told by Bertha Finn in the Anamosa centennial book, quoting Eureka editor Cliff Niles:

"He said, 'I do not know whether it can be done or not. I will go up with a 50-pound sack of sand and drop it. If it works, I will try 100 pounds, then 150 pounds.'

"So that afternoon he went up and dropped the sacks with no appreciable difficulty. He then signed the contract to make three drops at the Anamosa Fair.

"Everyone supposed they would practice it...when he arrived at the Fairgrounds he had a man with him whom he said would make the jump. When asked how he would make the jump from the plane, he said he was not sure, as he had never tried it. When the first day arrived, they went up in the air and flew around, but no parachute drop and finally landed. After much argument, they went up again and the parachute drop was made. To get away from the propeller, he had to jump from the end of the wing.

"The three jumps were made here, as per contract. The next week in Illinois, the wing broke from the plane and Max Lillie was killed.

"As far as we can find, this was the first drop in a parachute from a plane, ever made."

The fellow who jumped from the plane was Edgar F. "Mickey" McGurrin, who was known as the "Wild Irish Rose of the Air." He died in Grand Rapids, Michigan in 1959 at the age of 73.

Fans fill the stands and hillsides for racing in 1966.

Show Girls were always a big hit of the Fair.

Howard Suez' Elephants thrill audiences at the Fair.

well-known Monticello banker. A sportsman of the time was quoted in the Fair centennial booklet:

"Back in my baseball days 40 years ago, they used to take the ball on the first bounce, 15 feet back of the batter. Never knew such a thing as a mask and the boys used to take 'em in the bare hands like John L. and Jack Killian used to fight. This man Carpenter, he was considered the best ball catcher in these diggins and H.M., when the new-fangled face protector was invented, had the first one anyone had seen here-about.

"Well, when his team played at the Fair the first year with 'the catcher with the silver mask,' as they called him, people flocked from all over to see him. It was quite a sensation to have a man stand in the shadow of the batter and take the ball off the bat."

Free attractions at the 1903 Golden Jubilee Fair included "Aerial and Acrobatic Twins, Mystifying Feats, Laugh Provoking Knock-abouts, Thrilling Sensational Acts, Pleasing and Entertaining Diversities."

Then came airplanes, chorus lines, rodeos, Charleston contests, the "Gorgeous Girl" revue, the demolition derby, hay stacking, bale rolling, diaper derbies, chuckwagon races, alligator wrestling, bungee jumping, a greased pig scramble, and dozens of other events and attractions.

"I can remember years ago, there was a band that played every day," says Gail McNeill, "and a dog sat out on the track and barked at them the entire time."

"Everything closed at noon, even the Post Office," says Don Appleby, who has worked on the Fair for

(Continued on page 54)

High-wire acts kept people on the edge of their seats.

Baring and Daring

Lured by the barker's spiel, the men would stream down the hill as soon as the Fat Steer Show ended. It was a free show in the carnival's "girlie tent."

Don Appleby recalls, "They'd come down the Midway after Friday's Fat Steer Show to see the girls. When the show was over, the carnies would put the side of the tent up. You didn't go out the front — your wife might be there."

"Young men would slip into the tent and come face-to-face with their fathers," recalls Andy Anderson.

The barker's pitch was worse than the show, Don says. "It was worse on the outside than the inside — and it seems pretty tame by today's standards. We see worse than that on TV."

They were equal-opportunity barkers, at that. The women were urged to come in and see the show, too. "When we were young and single and working at the bank," says Ruth Harms, "we'd walk down the Midway and the barker would say, 'Come in and learn how to keep your husbands at home at night without home cookin'.'"

The
Miriam Sage
Dancers

years. "If you wanted a letter to go out, you had to mail it in the morning."

Some offerings have gained in popularity and have stayed with the Fair, while others have been left behind by the changing times. One innovation in the latter category was pari-mutuel betting. "That was our downfall," says former board member Cecil Goettsch. "We thought we had to have it. We planned for two years and spent a lot of money meeting state requirements. It lasted one year. We lost money and were glad to be out of it."

Another attraction from years past was the drawing for a new car. The first car was given away in 1938. "We backed off during the war years," says Cecil, "but we went back to it after the war and worked up to giving away five cars, one each night. At that time, a car cost $600 to $800 dollars."

"I can still remember the excitement of sitting in the box seat and watching them drive the cars in under the lights," says John Myers, "but I never won anything."

As cars became more and more costly, fewer were given away. Other prizes were added; they included bonds, cash awards of $1,000 and bicycles. When cars became just too expensive to be considered as prizes, the Fair switched to glamorous vacation trips — another big draw.

In 1983, a "free stage" was erected at the north end of the exhibits area, offering a better setting for free entertainment by local and area performers, and providing a place for Fairgoers to sit down.

Two cars and a pony were prizes at the Centennial Fair of 1953.

Marie Tobin stands in front of the car she won during the 1941 Fair.

Standing Up to Wartime Worries

People went about their business — as we're being urged to do today — and the Fair carried on through two world wars.

During World War I, decorations followed a patriotic motif and 4-H demonstrations emphasized food conservation — sugarless and wheatless meals as well as canning methods. Somehow, Candy Bill found enough sugar to make real taffy.

Twenty-five years later, "Food for Victory" was the theme. Fair buildings were decorated in red, white and blue. Navy recruiters were on the Midway, and carnival booths used Hitler and Hirohito as targets for baseball and shooting games.

There was renewed emphasis on canning and conservation; rationing severely limited sugar and other staples. A shortage of rubber for civilian use meant that rubber balls were missing from carnival games. Gasoline rationing limited driving, and the railroad restored passenger service from Cedar Rapids during Fair week.

Baseball games featured an Army team from Camp Grant and a Navy pre-flight team from Iowa City. The Great Lakes Blue Jackets, including legendary major-leaguers Johnny Mize and Mickey Cochrane, also played a Camp Grant team. Very few families were unaffected by the war, and the Fair was there to provide respite from their cares, distraction from their worries, and the support of friends and neighbors. New attendance records were set every day.

The 150th Great Jones County Fair once again plays this role: an extraordinary Fair for extraordinary times.

Attendance kept growing during the 1990s. Little Texas and the Budweiser Clydesdale team helped swell the numbers in 1994, when John Harms wrote, "This Fair will be one for the record books. A combination of great weather, great entertainment, a great crop in the field and a great attitude by everyone…made the event happen so well."

Sometimes the fairgoers got into the act: In 1995, 1,500 people, led by the All-Star Country Dancers, took to the track and tried to line-dance their way into the Guinness World Records book. There were thousands of people at the Fair that year, but not enough dancers; the effort to set a new record fell short by about 1,000.

In the past two years, another popular feature has been added to the Fair. Audiences enjoy the presentation of the Fair Queen. Any young woman can enter the competition, with the selection made by a panel of judges. The 2001 queen was Carrie Mardolf and the 2000 queen was Micaela Hogan.

Each of those two years set a new attendance record.

A comment that John Harms likes to challenge is, "Boy, you'll never get these kinds of crowds again!" or "You can't get this kind of entertainment here again!" John credits a hard-working Fair board for its commitment to top-notch entertainment and concession stands, and speaks glowingly of the role of young people who "will always be in the forefront."

"Maybe those people are right — maybe it can't be done," John says, "but we're going to try."

Nearly 100 years ago, when Roy Clark's Royal Scotch Highlanders Band headlined the Fair, patrons were told, "The best music is none too good for the Jones County Fair. This year the Fair Association goes clear 'over the top' in giving its patrons the best music money can buy. It spends more for music alone than many fairs spend for the entire line of attractions." Fairgoers can still count on "the best music money can buy" — probably not a Scottish bagpipe band. They know they'll see something new and different every year, and that most of their favorite

Lou Prohut makes the accordian sing in 1963.

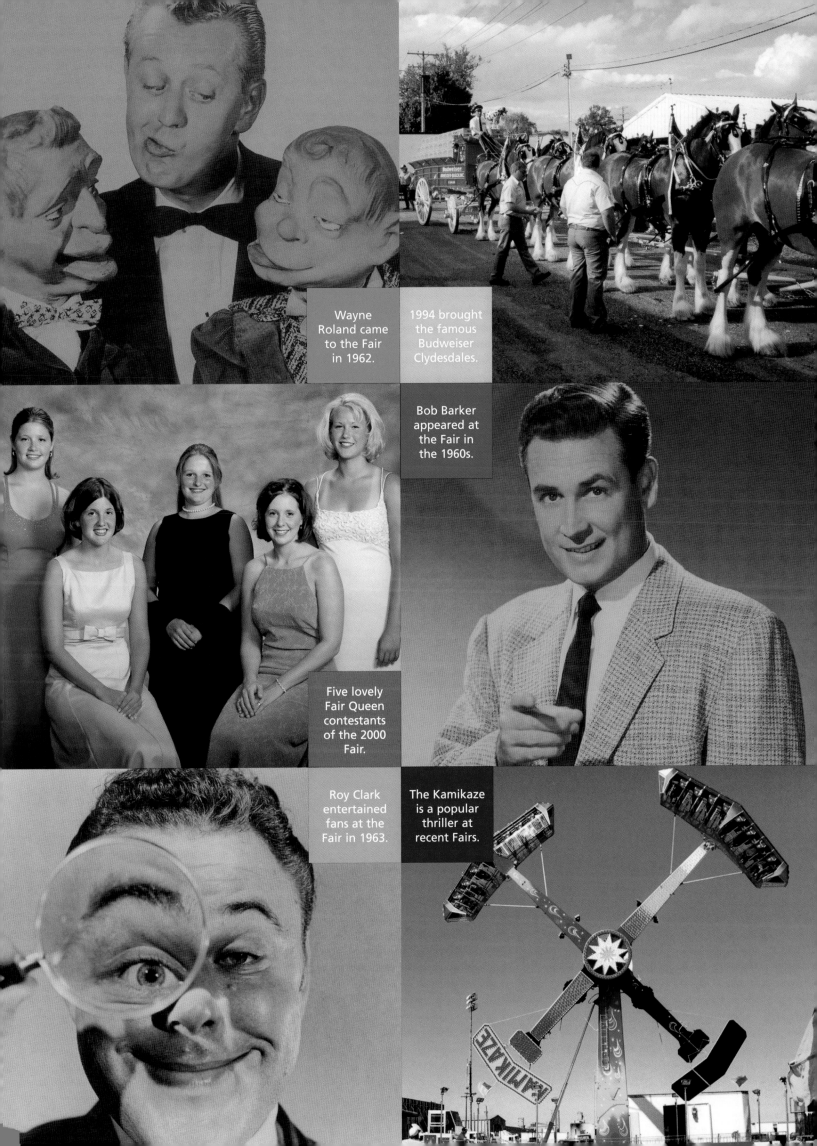

Wayne Roland came to the Fair in 1962.

1994 brought the famous Budweiser Clydesdales.

Bob Barker appeared at the Fair in the 1960s.

Five lovely Fair Queen contestants of the 2000 Fair.

Roy Clark entertained fans at the Fair in 1963.

The Kamikaze is a popular thriller at recent Fairs.

An Open Exhibit in Floral Hall circa 1930.

The "Reddy Kilowatt" exhibit keeps youngsters amused.

things from earlier years will be back.

A continuing part of the Fair, and one that echoes its original intent, is Open Exhibits. Those who take part can feel proud of their personal accomplishments; at the same time, their exhibits are a way of sharing their knowledge and skill with friends and neighbors. There is room for everyone here: dozens of classes with hundreds of categories and very few limitations.

The Floral Hall, constructed just after the Fair was moved from Anamosa to Monticello in 1874, was home to Open Exhibits for more than 80 years. Originally a round building with four wings, it was remodeled in 1941 and given a new, streamlined facade with two large wings. Then, in 1960, it was replaced with a

spacious tile and concrete Youth Center, which was remodeled in 1995 and renamed the Berndes Center. It serves the community's recreational and educational needs year-round, as well as being home to 4-H exhibits during Fair week.

Open Exhibits moved in 1964 to a new area — a brick shelter with a concrete floor just east of the Berndes Center. The shelter was constructed with removable wooden walls to allow it to be used as an exhibit hall during the Fair and a picnic shelter the rest of the year. Last year, it housed 1,500 entries, 400 more than the year before.

Pat Anderson, who has been superintendent of Open Exhibits for the past five years, is the person

Souvenir

CENTENNIAL FAIR

AUGUST 25-29

MONTICELLO IOWA

1853 - 1953

SOUVENIR OF THE GREAT JONES COUNTY FAIR...AUGUST 16-17-18-19–1950

THE GREAT JONES COUNTY FAIR . . . AUGUST 17 – 18 – 19 – 20 – 1949
THE BEAUTIFUL NATURAL FAIRGROUNDS, MONTICELLO, IOWA

FAIR GROUNDS ENTRANCE
...ICELLO. IOWA. 2-A-262

SOUVENIR OF THE JONES COUNTY FAIR, AUGUST 21-22-23–1946

LAMBERT'S SPORT SHOP — Tel. 353
Eastern Iowa's Largest Sporting Goods Store
MONTICELLO MASTERCRAFTS
Woodworking of all Kinds — Tel. 540
FREESE IMPLEMENT SALES — Tel. 477-W
Ford Tractor — Dearborn Farm Equipment.
FIRST'S ELECTRICAL SERVICE. — Tel 80
Contracting and Household Appliances
KURT'S KUBAN KAFE — Tel. 460
Home Made Pies and Short Orders
KURIGER BROTHERS — Tel. 311 W
Plumbing — Heating — Bendix Home Laundries

POST CARD

PLACE STAMP HERE
19 AT 52

...S BEAUTIFUL NATURAL FAIRGROUNDS, MONTICELLO, IOWA

Souvenir postcards from the Fair date back to 1912.

GAMBLE'S
WALL PAPER — PAINT — HARDWARE
Phone 237   Monticello, Iowa
G. M. JONES, Owner

POST CARD

Place Stamp Here

ICE COLD
ORANGEADE
LEMONADE
5¢   10¢

PAUSE...DRINK
Coca-Cola

Fresh
CARAMEL
CORN
10¢   5¢

The Fair is still a great place to find tasty treats and cold drinks.

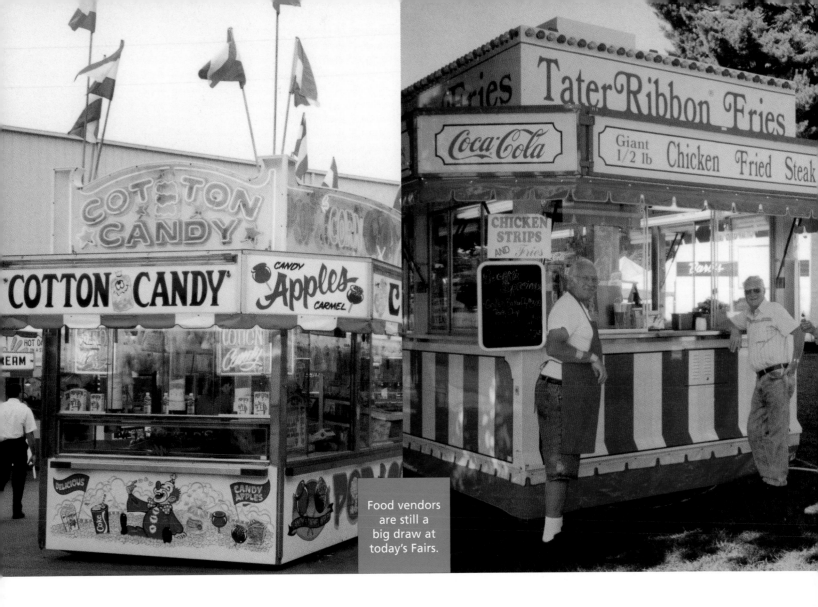

Food vendors are still a big draw at today's Fairs.

who coined the phrase, "The Five Best Days of Summer." It so captured the spirit of the Fair and of the community that it seems to be here to stay. "I don't know what made me think of it," Pat says, "except that for our family, the Fair has always been just that: the five best days of summer."

The Andersons have a long history with the Great Jones County Fair. Pat's husband, Andy, has been associated with it, in one capacity or another, for 45 years. He managed the Fair from 1989 until 1994,

when he turned those duties over to John Harms and agreed to help John by managing the concessions. Andy contracts with more than 30 vendors who make the Fair a memorable "food fest" each year.

Although there are no longer the nutsticks and cream candy of earlier days, the Lions Club stand remains a constant, serving a sit-down roast beef dinner and homemade pie. Other long-time vendors include Jeff Peterman of Marion, whose reputation for great tenderloins goes back 25 years, and Steve and Vicki

DUCK

BUGS BUNNY

PLUTO

All aboard!
Kids enjoy a
train ride
circa 1950.

Smith of Stratford, who have sold foot-long hot dogs at the Fair for 20 years.

Andy is also responsible for bringing in a top-notch carnival, Evans United Shows. The rides — especially the Kamikazi — are a favorite part of the Fair for many youngsters, who love the Midway.

Although the Fair is the five best days of summer, says Pat, "it takes 11 months to put it together." For Andy and Pat, that is time well spent. They enjoy being part of "bringing people together and having a good time for five days out of the year…to just relax and enjoy life."

New rides and exciting attractions are added each year.

The Magic of the Midway

For generations of Great Jones County Fairgoers, the Midway has been a magical place. The shrieks from the Tilt-a-Whirl, the tantalizing smell of the popcorn, the music of the merry-go-round — all combine to cast their spell.

It takes more management than magic, however, to create a successful Midway. According to Fair manager John Harms, only the best business people survive. There are only about 500 carnival operators in the entire country, and not enough in Iowa for every fair and festival to have one. John feels fortunate to have Evans United Shows at the Great Jones County Fair.

The Evans Shows began in 1947, when Bill, Don and Jim Evans came home to Kansas City after serving in the army in World War II. With their parents, Clay and Pearl Evans, they bought a train ride and a chair swing, and went on the road. The train was dubbed the "Sunshine Choo Choo," and featured a live monkey in the engineer's cab.

From this small beginning the show has grown to become one of the largest in the Midwest, with a huge rolling fleet of trucks and trailers. Tom Evans and his wife, Nancy, now own and manage the show. Tom is Bill's son, and a third-generation carnival operator. Nancy taught first and second grades for 25 years, spending her summers with the carnival. They have two daughters. Erin, 24, a radiology catscan technologist, helps with the carnival whenever she can. Emily, 21, a college junior majoring in elementary education, still spends her summers running the cotton candy and popcorn trailer.

The carnival has been a great place to raise the children, Nancy says. "We're all together, and the kids grow up with a good work ethic. Our work generates a sense of pride. Everything looks nice, and people have fun."

Evans United Shows first came to the Great Jones County Fair in 1982 and 1983. After that, scheduling conflicts kept the show away until 1994, when Andy Anderson succeeded in re-establishing the relationship. Evans has provided the Midway every year since then.

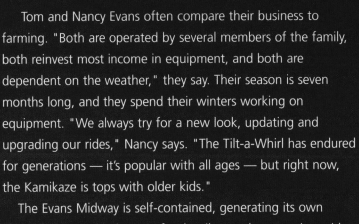

Tom and Nancy Evans often compare their business to farming. "Both are operated by several members of the family, both reinvest most income in equipment, and both are dependent on the weather," they say. Their season is seven months long, and they spend their winters working on equipment. "We always try for a new look, updating and upgrading our rides," Nancy says. "The Tilt-a-Whirl has endured for generations — it's popular with all ages — but right now, the Kamikaze is tops with older kids."

The Evans Midway is self-contained, generating its own electricity, operating its own food trailers and contracting with independent owners of games. The show carries its own bunk houses and provides bunks and showers for its employees, many of whom have been with the carnival for years.

"A lot of people had their roots in this business," Nancy says. That includes Ed McMahon, Johnny Carson's "Tonight Show" sidekick and a former carnival pitchman who sold products at shows and fairs. Years ago, the shows brought many "acts" to the Midway, spectator forms of entertainment that could not be seen anywhere else. Today, rides are the main attraction in a business that has changed with the times.

It seems likely that the partnership between the Evans Shows and the Great Jones County Fair will bring an outstanding Midway to Monticello for years to come. "We have such a good relationship with the Great Jones County Fair that they have provided shirts for our crew with both the Evans logo and the Fair logo on them," says Nancy. "In our 32 weeks on the road, this is the only fair that does that."

The Evans people contribute to that relationship by providing a special "early opening" for Camp Courageous. "Our employees always seem to 'step up' that day to be their best and to be helpful," Nancy says.

"We look forward to coming to Monticello each year. It's a great fair run by great folks."

A busy ticket booth on the Fair Midway

SCOOT

SAFETY

1. KEEP HANDS & ARMS INSIDE CAR
2. KEEP SHOULDER STRAP ON
3. AVOID HEAD ON COLLISION

4. STA RI
5. YO

ACCOM
6. OP
ANY

15

Big kids and little kids all love the bumper cars.

LeAnn Rimes. Tanya Tucker. Martina McBride. Marie Osmond. Johnny Cash. Reba McIntyre. Loretta Lynn. Barbara Mandrell. The Statler Brothers. Alabama. Tommy Sands. Tex Ritter. Styx.

THE ENTERTAINERS

They've all appeared at the Great Jones County Fair, along with dozens of other stars. In fact, says Gail McNeill, these big-name performers represent the biggest change in the Fair during the past 50 years.

Gail knows about such things. She has researched and written the history of the Fair in "A Century of Progress," a booklet produced for the Fair's centennial, and "The Great Jones County Fair," which is included in "Monticello, 1836-1986," a book commemorating the sesquicentennial of Monticello. Her husband, Albert H. McNeill, served on the Fair board for many years.

"TV and popular culture drive the Fair," Gail says. "It's fascinating the way the Fair changes in response to what people want."

What people wanted in the 1930s was circus acts and variety shows, many of them a take-off on vaudeville, according to Glenn Lambert, who admits to being associated with the Fair, in one way or another, since the mid-1920s. His father, R.C. Lambert, was a board member, and Glenn followed in his footsteps, serving on the board from 1971 to 1987. He remembers that "we always had a high aerial act here."

"The stage shows went from variety reviews to bigger shows put on by one entertainer, such as Harry James," Glenn says. And there were chorus lines — some of the girls deeply tanned and others ashen white.

LeAnn
Rimes
1997

Johnny Cash and June Carter Cash 1987

Waylon Jennings 1993

Jerry Clower 1997

Grand Funk Railroad 1997

Charlie
Daniels
1991

Martina
McBride
1999

"Today, it's stars," Glenn says. Cecil Goettsch, another long-time Fair board member, agrees. "There have been so many changes in the Fair, it's unbelievable," he says. The biggest change has been the acts."

Years ago, however, there was another change that made "star acts" possible. It was outdoor lighting.

Try to imagine a Fair that ends each day at six o'clock. It would be like a cake without frosting. But in the days before street lights and Daylight Savings Time, that's exactly what happened.

Fair officials tried to help this situation by moving Fair dates up to early August in 1899 and 1900, to take advantage of longer daylight hours. They managed to extend the hours of the Fair, but lost some attendance.

The next year, the dates went back to late August.

After dark, Fairgoers went to the Opera House downtown, where companies were always engaged for nightly performances during Fair week. "Camille" and "Secrets of the Police in Russia" broke box office records in the early years of the 20th century.

All that changed in 1915, when electroliers were installed on the grounds and in the amphitheater. A Night Fair and a Night Carnival came into being — with patrons assured that gasoline lanterns were ready, just in case. Audiences heard band concerts and saw vaudeville, and found the "star quality" of the entertainers growing each year. Glenn and Cecil not only watched this happen, but had a role in

Travis
Tritt
2001

Tanya
Tucker
1989 & 2001

bringing it about.

Cecil's story begins in 1937: "I came to Monticello on July 6. Nine days later I was recruited to be part of a caravan to go to surrounding towns to advertise the Fair. We ended up at a home in Dubuque where we played nickel poker and ate pickles out of a big barrel."

He was later asked to join the Fair board, and was put in charge of the amphitheater in 1941. The evening entertainment consisted of band concerts and circus acts, with a chorus line between acts. Fewer than half of the box seats were sold, at a cost of $3 for the entire Fair, and there were no reserved seats. "We rented the folding chairs," Cecil says, "and at the conclusion of the Fair, there would be 25 to 50 chairs missing. That was

when the chains and padlocks were purchased."

The amphitheater had been built in 1902 at a cost of $4,000. In 1918, the boxes were rebuilt on concrete piers, and the stalls were divided into compartments large enough to hold four chairs. Those concrete piers were all that was left after a fire destroyed the wooden structure in 1930, just three weeks before the Fair. The Fair Association quickly erected a temporary structure. The amphitheater on the Anamosa Fairgrounds burned the same year and was never rebuilt, ending the Anamosa Fair.

As a board member, Cecil helped preview and contract with entertainers. "The International Exposition was held the first week of December and

(Continued on page 74)

Splintered and broken sticks left by famous high-energy drummers.

John
Michael
Montgomery
2001

they compare favorably with any other Fair facilities now."

There have been many other changes, as well. Fifty years ago, box seats (four chairs) sold for three dollars, and were only 40 percent sold. Today, boxes cost $100 and are all sold out. (There's even a waiting list — when a box becomes available, a lottery decides who will have the opportunity to buy it.) For that $100, four people get to see 10 events during Fair week —

$2.50 for each person for each event.

But if you think that's a bargain, listen to what Pat Anderson has to say: "For just $6, you can park your car, get into the Fair, and take advantage of everything that's offered — including the mainstage show. You can sit on the hillside and see and hear everything."

Maybe that's what really makes the Great Jones County Fair "Great."

Billy Ray
Cyrus
1999

Jody
Miller
1971

Lori
Morgan
1990

David Lee
Murphy
1997

Eddie
Burnette
and Yvonne
1962

How Did He Do That?

Then there was the magician who put his daughter in a woven basket on one side of the stage, and made her emerge from another basket on the other side of the stage. How did he do that? Don Appleby discovered that the daughter had a twin, and the twin had spent the entire afternoon curled up in the second basket, waiting to emerge during the evening performance.

Concert and Date Both First-Rate

The date was August 9, 1980. The event was the Nitty Gritty Dirt Band concert at the Great Jones County Fair. This was the when and where of my first date with Brian Manternach, a Jones County 4-Her. I remember that the concert was great, even though it rained later in the evening.

The date was the first of many for us; five years later, we were married. Now, with our five children, we farm in Jones County. Our children are just joining 4-H, so we are able to celebrate our wedding anniversary, July 20th, watching them participate in the livestock shows at the Fair.

Thanks for the memories, Jones County Fair!

LuAnn Demmer Manternach

A Kiss is Just a Kiss...

But it's remembered for years when it comes from Anita Bryant.

Eli Shada was sitting in his box, watching her show, when she called him up on the stage for a dance. Afterward, she gave him a kiss. This particular evening in 1964 stands out in Eli's memory even more than the famed Statler Brothers show, which drew record crowds.

A Fair board member for "25 or 30 years," Eli also has fond memories of his board service. "We had a good old time," he says. "We worked hard, but we had a lot of fun."

Merle
Haggard
Live at the
Fair, 1994

Entertainment at The Great Jones County Fair – 1956 to 2001

1956 Tex Ritter, Smiley Barnett, Ray Anthony Orchestra, Charlie Spivak Orchestra

1957 Don Rogers, Jeffery Clay, Sammy Kay, Candy Candido

1958 Ted Weems, Homer & Jethro, Herb Schriner, Eddy Peabody & Teddy Phillips, Four Preps, Alvin & The Chipmunks

1959 Tommy Sands & Ben Beri, Edgar Bergen & Charlie McCarthy, Alvin & Chipmunks

1960 Bob Crosby, June Taylor Dancers, Brenda Lee

1961 Neil Sedaka, Frankie Masters, Abbott & Costello, Candy Candido

1962 Glenn Miller Orchestra by Tex Beneke, Ray Eberle, Skitch Henderson

1963 Glenn Miller Orchestra by Ray McKinley, Jimmy Durren, Peter Palmer Orchestra

1964 Jerry Van Dyke, Conway Twitty, Anita Bryant, Grandpa Jones

1965 George Kirby, Judy Miller, Bobby Burgess, Barbara Boylan, Roger Miller, Johnny Tillotson

1966 Ferlin Husky, Peter Drake, Ronnie Dove, Buffalo Bill

1967 Bobby Vinton, George Kirby, Porter Wagonner, Allen Rossi

1968 Rex Allen, Minnie Pearl, Skitch Henderson, Faron Young, Statler Brothers, Stony Mt. Cloggers

1969 Ferlin Husky, Carl Perkins, Pat Butram, Burgess & King, Jimm Darrow

1970 Sonny James, Barbara Mandrell, Golddiggers

1971 Ray Price, Jodi Miller, Conway Twitty, Oak Ridge Boys, George Kirby

Anita
Bryant
1964

1972 Bobby Vinton, Boots Randolph, Jerry Van Dyke

1973 Statler Brothers, Frankie Carr, Frankie Avalon

1974 Kids Next Door, Clay Hart, Mel Tillis, Ray Stevens

1975 David Houston, Lorretta Lynn, Porter Wagonner

1976 Ronnie Milsap, Judy Lynn, Marty Robbins

1977 Sonny James, Bobby Goldsburo, Lorretta Lynn

1978 Bob McGrath of Sesame Street, Statler Brothers, Flash Cadillac

1979 Grandpa Jones, Oak Ridge Boys, Kingston Trio, Jim Ed Brown

1980 Tanya Welk, Lorretta Lynn, Nitty Gritty Dirt Band, Chubby Checker

1981 Johnny Cash, Alabama, Helen Cornelius

1982 Box Car Willie, Pure Prairie League, Sylvia & the Challengers

1983 Roy Clark, Lettermen, T.G. Sheppard, Jeanne C. Riley

1984 Ronnie McDowell, Nitty Gritty Dirt Band, Louise Mandrell, The Kendals

1985 Reba McEntire, Sawyer Brown, Jerry Reed, Atlanta, Ronny Robbins

1986 The Memories, Dave & Sugar, Exile, Mel McDaniel, Life

1987 Bellamy Brothers, Ricky Skaggs, Johnny Cash, June Carter Cash

1988 Micky Gilley, Marie Osmond, Highway 101

1989 Tanya Tucker, Eddie Rabbitt, Sha Na Na

1990 Nitty Gritty Dirt Band, Lorrie Morgan, Shenandoah, The Diamonds, Johnny Tillotson, Brian Hyland, Hot Rod Chevy Band

Reba
McEntire
1985

Roger
Miller
1965

Neil
Sedaka
1961

Ty
England
1996

Homer
and Jethro
1958

Patty
Loveless
1991

Michelle
Wright
1993

1991 Charlie Daniels, Patty Loveless, Marty Stuart

1992 Mark Chesnutt, Tracy Lawrence, Trisha Yearwood

1993 Michelle Wright, Waylon Jennings, Chris LeDoux, McBride & The Ride

1994 Confederate Railroad, Doug Supernaw, Little Texas, Merle Haggard, Twister Alley

1995 The Tractors, Ken Mellons, The Kentucky Headhunters, Ronnie McDowell, Lee Greenwood

1996 John Anderson, Ty England, 38 Special

1997 LeAnn Rimes, David Lee Murphy, Grand Funk Railroad, Jerry Clower, Mustang Sally

1998 Neal McCoy, The Oak Ridge Boys, Three Dog Night, Starship

1999 BTO Band, Billy Ray Cyrus, Martina McBride, Little River Band

2000 Alabama, Lila McCann, Kenny Chesney, Sawyer Brown

2001 Tanya Tucker, Travis Tritt, Styx, Jessica Andrews, Billy Gilman, John Michael Montgomery

2002 Toby Keith, George Jones, Aaron Tippin, Lynyrd Skynyrd, Steve Holy, Leroy VanDyke, The Vogues, RPM

Some have followed in their fathers' footsteps. Some were recruited by friends. Some serve on the board. Some make up the dozens of Fair-week volunteers. Some farm, some live in town. All love the Fair.

MAKING IT HAPPEN

Andy Anderson is one of those who was "recruited" to work on the Fair. That was 45 years ago, and he's been doing it ever since.

"When I first came to town to teach in the high school, Boyd Shannon was gate manager. He put me to work selling tickets to the cars lined up along Maple Street to get into the Fair.

"The next year, Boyd said, 'Well, you didn't make any mistakes, so you can come inside now and be the assistant gate manager.'

"Then a couple of years later, he said, 'You know what goes on — now you can be ticket manager.' I was ticket manager for 29 or 30 years, then Al Westhoff (who had been manager of the Fair) left, and the board said, 'You're the only one who's been around long enough, in and out of the office,

to know what's been going on, so you've got to become the manager.'

"Well, I wasn't quite sure I knew all the ins and outs, but I did manage the Fair for six years or so. Then I developed prostate cancer, and asked for some help. John Harms worked with me for a year, and then took over as manager. I thought 'Now I can just take it easy and sit in my box that I've never sat in.' But John told me I couldn't leave — I had to be concession manager. So here I am."

Andy's 45-year history with the Fair puts him in a class with Cecil Goettsch, who started promoting the Fair to Eastern Iowans just nine days after arriving in Monticello in 1937; Glenn Lambert, whose board service from 1971 to 1987 followed in the footsteps of his father, R.C. Lambert; and Don

Volunteers are a huge part of the Fair's success.

Fairgrounds
entrance
circa 1912

Fairgrounds
entrance
circa 1920

C. J. Matthiessen, Head of Fair Police circa 1938

Monticello Park entrance circa 1908

The park fountain circa 1940

Appleby, whose father, Claude Appleby, also served on the Fair board for many years.

"The Fair has always been a big part of my family's life," says Glenn. That was also true in the Appleby family. Don remembers summers as a kid, when the family project was pouring cement into forms to make the parking lot posts. "They were white cement, about six inches square and pointed on top," says Don. "My dad was in charge of the Fairgrounds, and we made hundreds of them over several summers. Oh, how I hated those posts!"

Don's early experiences didn't keep him from a long association with the Fair. He has been a stagehand, concession manager and assistant Fair manager, among other varied responsibilities — such as transporting celebrities from their hotels to the Fair. "When Tommy Sands was here," Don recalls, "Dewie Gesie and I had to go out to Eden's and get him. Tommy wanted a

Highway Patrol escort with sirens running, but what he got was Dewie's old coupe."

Both Glenn and Don have been honored with "Friend of the Fair" status, an award that recognizes consistent support and effort toward the success of the Fair. Cecil was named to the Fair's Hall of Fame in 1994, and Glenn was honored in 1996.

If there had been a Hall of Fame in earlier times, other prominent Jones County people would also be on that list. Many records of Fair boards and leadership have been lost through the years. There are some long-ago names, however, that do keep appearing on records that survive: Matthiessen, Locher, Carpenter, Stuhler, Iverson, Shover, Hoag, Rodman and Hogan are among them.

Since 1987, when the Fair was reorganized into a publicly owned entity, a complete record of board members has been kept. That reorganization, with its

(Continued on page 104)

Friends of the Fair

Since its inception in 1989, the "Friend of the Fair" award
has honored seven organizations and six individuals for their
contributions to the success of the Great Jones County Fair.

They are:

1989	KLEH Radio
1990	Kromminga Motors
1991	Andy Anderson
1992	Ray Kleinow
1993	Glenn Lambert
1994	Al Westhoff
1995	Don Appleby
1996	Duane Mesch
1997	Dale Lee Distributing
1998	Monticello Express
1999	N & N Trailer
2000	Lasso-E Camper Sales
2001	Jones County Farm Bureau

Taking the Plunge

Many things are expected of the Fair board president, but bungee jumping isn't one of them. Nevertheless, at the 1992 Fair, John Harms took it upon himself to demonstrate that the jump was safe. Tethered by his ankles, he took the plunge and lived to tell the story. John doesn't like heights — he's uncomfortable even standing on a picnic table — but he was convinced that it was safe to make the jump, and he wanted to demonstrate that to Fairgoers.

When Marilyn Streeper succeeded John as board president, a local reporter asked her if she intended to make a jump. Marilyn chose, instead, an activity more in keeping with the origin and spirit of the Fair. She earned the crowd's applause by leading a three-person penning team demonstration.

Present and past Fair managers, John Harms and Andy Anderson

elected and representative board, brought sweeping change to the Fair. Al Westhoff, who had previously served on the board, was manager at the time. He was instrumental in bringing about the change that actually saved the Fair. John Harms tells the story:

"Al could see that there was a real problem with the direction in which the Fair was heading. Enthusiasm was dying, public support was leaving and there was a $50,000 debt. Something had to be done. Al got the idea to sell the golf course property, develop a 10-year cash flow, and turn the board into a publicly elected group from all over the county. The concept was Al's. He was the key to the turnaround."

Al recalls, "I knew if we were to get this done at all, we had to pay back the bank. I was on the city council and I went to talk to the mayor about our debt. We owned 137 acres. The city owned 40 acres, right in the middle of it. The golf course didn't own any land — they leased it. The city owned part of the golf club and the Fair owned the other part. So we kept five acres and sold the rest to the city and the golf club, and we got enough cash to pay back the bank.

"It had to be done — we were going backwards. There was a stigma attached to the Fair; it wasn't seen as broad-based. There were people who lived right

$5.00 bought one share of Fair stock in 1925.

across the street who wouldn't go to the Fair. We couldn't have survived more than another two years.

"We reorganized, going from a nonprofit stock corporation to a county fair. We gave the Fair to the county."

The new board represented every district in the county, returning the Fair to its agricultural base. "That's what the Fair is all about," says Glenn, who supported the change as a member of the "old board," and continued to serve as a member of the new board. "It's about 4-H and agriculture." The board also includes representatives of the entities having interests in the Fair: city and county government, the golf club, the extension service, 4-H, and beef, dairy and pork groups.

Al's plan was put into effect. The stigma was overcome. But Al knew he had to leave, because, he says, "I was part of the old stigma, and it was time for me to move on." Not an easy thing to do, for someone who hadn't missed a Great Jones County Fair in 50 years. But, Al says, "I loved the Fair business and I wanted to go into it full-time. I enjoyed every part of the job — I enjoyed going to work every single day. I still do."

Now the full-time manager of the Josephine County

The Fair
grandstand
and oval track
circa 1916

Fair in Oregon, Al has been a model for John. "Al was the one who gave me the fire for the business," John says. "I had the Fair background as an exhibitor, but he gave me the desire to be on the board, to get into management."

It's easy to see that John shares Al's enthusiasm for his work. The part-time managerial position he holds is rarely that. "You work on the Fair 12 months of the year," says John. "People come in the week after the Fair and ask us what we're going to do, now that the Fair's over. We're already working on the next Fair. We work half-time six months of the year, and time-and-a-half the other six months."

The board and staff are guided by the *mission statement* they have adopted: "Our mission is to continue the rich tradition of the Great Jones County

Fair, and to provide educational and competitive opportunities for our Fairgoers. We also are committed to promoting the finest entertainment features that we can justify, while still maintaining unmatched value to area events. Our agricultural roots must never be forgotten in the quest of this mission."

Today, the Great Jones County Fair is financially successful. That, too, can be dangerous, says John. "When everyone understood the Fair was struggling, many people gave time and effort. We don't want to lose that kind of support, so the board puts every-thing we make back into the Fair, constantly upgrading facilities and bringing outstanding entertainment."

"It's never shabby," echoes Marilyn Streeper, a past president. "We've worked hard to get things that were needed, improving rest rooms and livestock barns

(Continued on page 110)

Hall of Fame

Lifetime contributions to the Great Jones County Fair have been recognized since 1990 by election to the Hall of Fame. The Hall of Fame roll includes:

1990	Sam Rhatigan	1994	Cecil Goettsch	1998	Glenn Tobiason
1991	James A. Maurice	1995	Dewie Gesie	1999	Eli Shada
1992	Claude Appleby	1996	Glenn Lambert	2000	Ed Helgens
1993	Joe Legg	1997	Sam Schuetz	2001	Varlyn Fink

Jones County Fair Association

1853 Eighty=seventh Year 1940

August 20=21=22=23
1940

"Iowa's Most Beautiful Fairgrounds"

Monticello, Iowa

BOARD of DIRECTORS

M. T. Stott - M. F. Hogan - W. R. Zubler
C. D. Shaffer - C. Grafft - J. J. Locher
H. W. Stuhler - H. M. Carpenter, Jr.
C. J. Matthiessen - M. A Wortman
C. A. McLaughlin - R. C. Lambert
H. I. Rodman - A. J. Stuhler
J. A. Maurice

OFFICERS

H. W. Stuhler	President
H. M. Carpenter, Jr.	Vice President
J. A. Maurice	Treasurer
H. I. Rodman	Secretary
W. R. Zubler	Concessions
C. D. Shaffer	
M. T. Stott	Speed Superintendents

January, 16, 1941

Mr. Marvin Jansen
Anamosa, Iowa

Dear Friend Marvin:

We wish to thank you for the large part you have
had in making the Jones County Fair one of the leading Fairs in Iowa.
Upon checking the State records, I find we rank 5th in gate receipts.
This does not exclude Waterloo, Spencer, Marshalltown or Davenport.
What an enviable record this is, which you can help us rejoice in.
The 4-H Clubs of Jones County have done much
to make our Fair a success, and is fast becoming recognized as
one of the best Counties in Iowa.
There is a lot of work, worry, and financial
risk in putting on a Fair. We some times wonder whether it is
worth the effort, but when we receive such letters of appreciation
you boys have sent us, we take a new grip, and are determined to
truly make it "Bigger and Better" again this ...
We staked ... when we
decided to go to st...
among ...

---

air Association

...MAN, Secretary
...llo, Iowa

MONTICELLO
JAN 16
5 30 PM
1941
IOWA

UNITED
STATES POSTAG...
2 CENTS

Mr. Marvin Jansen,

Anamosa, Iowa.

20 = 23, 1940
Beautiful Grounds in the State

A view from above: the '94 Great Jones County Fair Midway

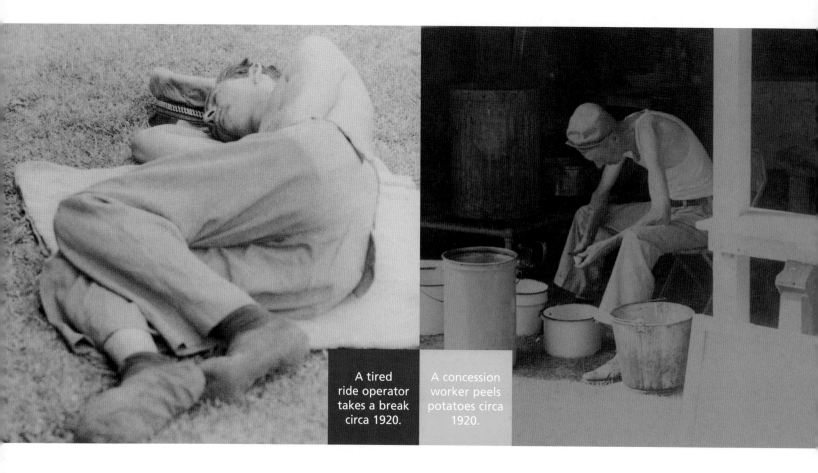

A tired ride operator takes a break circa 1920.

A concession worker peels potatoes circa 1920.

and all the grounds. We put the money right back into the Fair."

Serving on the Fair board isn't easy. There's a lot of physical work to be done, and everyone pitches in. It starts in the spring, with the annual kickoff event — a barbecue for all the sponsors, contributors, and volunteers. The menu combines the products of the pork, dairy and beef commodity groups of the county: bacon cheeseburgers.

Then there's promotion, which takes board members all over northeast Iowa. "We do a lot of parades," says Marilyn, "and events like Hiawatha's 'Hog Wild Days.' We have people line dancing on a flat bed pulled by John's truck." Joe Yedlik says, "You don't have to build a new float for every parade, or stuff napkins into chicken wire. You put your banner on there, and it's

clean and it's loud."

When Fair week comes, the real work begins. "Board members are there, working, not sitting in an office," John says. "They wear the white shirts with the Fair logo, so people know who they are. If we all can be out there working and sweating and getting our white shirts dirty — with smiles on our faces — people are going to pick up on that. They'll know we're having a good time."

Marilyn agrees. "We all have a good time working together. And when people tell you they really enjoyed the Fair, it's a good feeling. I think everybody on the board has that feeling. It's fun working together. It's fun to come early, get the barns ready — I can hardly wait to get the flags up!"

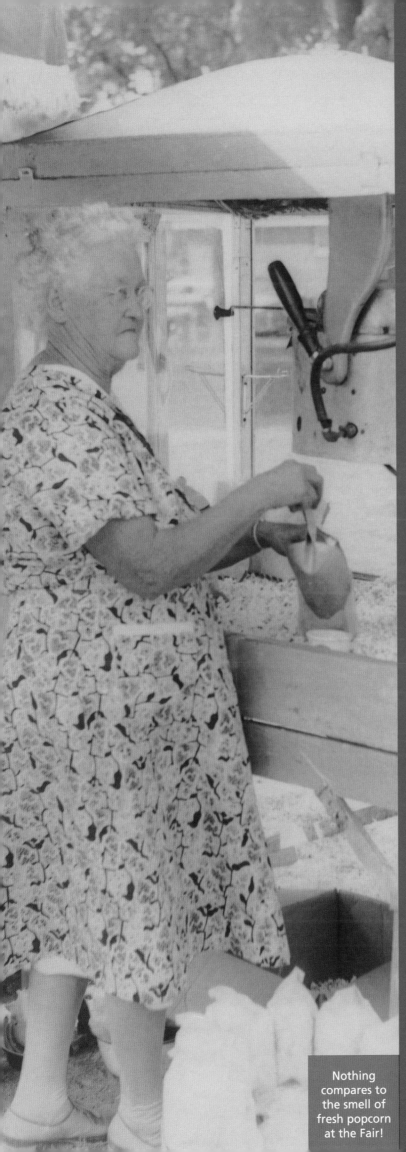

Nothing compares to the smell of fresh popcorn at the Fair!

Working for the Fair

During the past 15 years, more than 75 people have served on the Great Jones County Fair board. They have represented the entire county, and have helped the Fair return to its agricultural base. At the same time, they have created a Fair that offers "something for everyone" and draws people from neighboring states as well as Eastern Iowa.

They have put the Fair on firm financial footing, building on an annual allocation of a little more than $19,000 from the county. The Fair also receives about $10,000 from the state, its share of the $7 million the legislature appropriates annually to support Iowa's county fairs. They've plowed the profits right back into the Fair, improving facilities and bringing in high-quality entertainment.

They've worked hard, and they've had fun doing it.
They are:

Ralph Anderson	Jim Hogan	Kevin Prull
Bud Bader	Jim Holt	Bruce Reade
Kevin Bergman	Fred Iben	Sam Rhatigan
Jim Blythe	Linda Kahler	Gary Rickels
Russell Brown	Lolly Kurt	Rex Rickels
Eugene Brunscheen	Rich Knepper	Dean Ricklefs
Shirlee Brunscheen	Richmond	Donna Robinson
Rich Burmahl	Kromminga	Wayne Robinson
John	Glenn Lambert	Mike Secrist
Christopherson	Dan Lambertson	Dennis Shoop
Leo Cook	Joe Legg	Steve Strang
Dennis Coon	Al Lubben	Marilyn Streeper
Greg Covington	Marvin Manternach	Mike Streeper
Joe Cruise	Brian McQuillen	Kyle Tapken
Bob Davis	Dennis McDermott	Jani Telleen
Jack Dietiker	Kevin Miller	Bill Tenley
Mike Dirks	Garrett Moenk	Leo Tjaden
Keith Dirks	Douglan Monck	Glenn Tobiason
Dana Edwards	Jeff Monck	Gary Toenjes
Don Eilers	Merlyn Moore	Ryan Toenjes
Russ Engelbart	Keith Morningstar	Miles Treadway
John Frasher	Ron Nowachek	Paul Wagner
Phil Gerdes	Joann Paulson	Delbert Weber
Joe Green	Don Peters	Keith Wenndt
John Harms	Marty Pitzel	Vance Wickham
Don Hardersen	Mike Plueger	Merlyn Wilken
Wendy Heeren	Ray Poppe	Richard Wolken

SOUVENIR OF THE JONES COUNTY FAIR . . . AUGUST 20-21-22—1947
NATURE'S BEAUTIFUL NATURAL FAIRGROUNDS, MONTICELLO, IOWA

BUILDINGS & GROUNDS CHRONOLOGY

1874
Union Driving Park Association moved the Fair from Anamosa to its 40 acres at Monticello and borrowed $1,800 to erect the Floral Hall.

1883
Association improved buildings, pumped well water from city grounds; constructed sidewalk from train depot.

1891
City purchased the 40-acre Fairground.

1902
Fair Association newly incorporated, issued $3,000 of stock, paid dividends for several years; constructed $4,000 amphitheater and graded track.

1915
Electric outdoor lighting installed.

1918
Boxes rebuilt.

1919
New swine pavilion added with cement floor and running water; parking on grounds.

1920
Special 70-foot stage constructed for H.M.S. Pinafore production.

1930
Amphitheater burned; temporary grandstand constructed on old foundation.

1939
Racing stables built, $2,500.

1941
New wings added to the Floral Hall.

1944
New pens and bleachers added for Fat Steer Show.

1944-45
Association purchased three acres (Clark's Lots) just east of Country Club; took an option on (later purchased) Bajasch property, 33 acres east of race track, for parking area and golf course; constructed large brick women's rest room; built dormitory on old poultry building foundation.

Jones County
Fairgrounds
in 1906

Pens and judging area circa 1950

1951
New administration building incorporated part of the old brick ticket office at the main gate; included first aid and hospital unit, lost and found department, information center, public telephones, administrative and ticket offices.

1952
Hollow north of amphitheater filled in to seat overflow crowds and allow people to see stage. Free Stage enlarged; modern drinking fountains, new blacktop street from main gate to 4-H barns added.

1957
New baseball lunch stand, portable steel pens installed for Fat Steer Show.

1960
Youth Center replaced the Floral Hall; horse barn burned down.

1961
New horse barn constructed.

1964
Brick picnic shelter/exhibit hall built.

1967
Drive to golf club paved.

1970
New all-steel amphitheater, constructed with steel bleachers and roof; seating capacity increased by a third.

1971
New exhibition barn for livestock shows put show ring and bleachers under cover.

1983
New Free Stage and seating added. New guard rail installed on track.

1987
The big transition. The Fair, the City of Monticello, and the Monticello Golf Board entered into agreements to reorganize property ownership and develop the plan

Judges atop the fence of the new pen area circa 1945.

that improved the future of all involved. Much of the property that was owned by the Fair, but provided no cash flow, was sold to the other two entities and leased back to the Fair.

1988

A rectangular picnic shelter was constructed on the fairgrounds by the Lutheran Brotherhood to provide an additional sheltered area during the Fair, and for the city park during the rest of the year.

1989

A number of repairs were made to the amphitheater. Drainage was improved away from the seating areas, and a number of concrete walls were corrected. Several steps were replaced and installed.

1993

A major capital campaign was launched across the county, and enough money was raised to construct a livestock pavilion to house dairy, beef, and horses during different parts of the Fair. This building was

built large enough to tie the livestock for their stay, with areas to groom and prepare for the show rings. A big feature of the building was to over-kill the electrical service to satisfy the increasing needs of the exhibitors.

1994

The outside horse show ring was increased in size by one-third, and the perimeter rail and posts were replaced with maintenance-free recycled materials.

1995

Several areas of new concrete sidewalks and approaches were replaced as part of an ongoing repair program around the grounds.

The Berndes Family Trust, Homeland Bank, the City of Monticello, the Monticello Community Schools, and the Fair began an extensive study to improve the Youth Center on the grounds. Plans included an expansion of a 9000-square-foot addition to include meeting rooms, workout areas, locker rooms, showers,

(Continued on page 118)

Fairground
race track
area circa
1950

Styx performs live in the upgraded amphitheater in 2001.

and a completely refurbished multipurpose room for any type of event. The plan included a vote by the public to bond for about half of the needed funding. The vote failed, and the "Plan B" was implemented. The down-scaled version remodeled the existing structure, and was designed to accommodate the additional features if needed. This new building was then changed in name from the "Youth Center," to the "Monticello Berndes Center," or "MBC." This was then the home for the commercial exhibits, and the 4-H exhibits during the Fair.

A seven-year plan was adopted to re-side the old dairy barn with steel, new overhead doors, ventilation doors, and vents. The decision was to repair one face at a time.

The main office of the Fair was gutted and three interior rooms were developed into one large, more efficient office. A ceiling with brighter lighting was installed, and the office was carpeted. The cost of the improvements was met by private donations.

The week after the Fair, a tornado ripped through the north end of Monticello and the Fairgrounds. Many trees were destroyed, power lines were down, and many of the buildings sustained damage. The cleanup and

repair lasted about a month. All new windows were built and installed on the horse barn.

1996
Second year of old dairy barn repair.

Various electrical improvements were made.

1997
New stage. LeAnn Rimes was coming and we had to do something! The whole stage was destroyed, then rebuilt. It was moved back to accommodate more seating on the track, and improve the movement of equipment on the stage. The result was an additional thousand seats on the track, making the concert environment more attractive for larger and more elaborate productions. This development also included an expanded electrical service to the dressing rooms and power for the tour busses.

Third year of improvements of old dairy barn.

1998
New electrical service provided for the camping vehicles and tour busses in the "back stage" compound.

Fourth year of new siding on the old dairy barn.

Outside the new barn areas, 1996

The four sides are now complete, with six overhead doors and about 20 ventilation doors installed.

The old air conditioner in the office died. A new high-efficiency unit was installed.

Speaker towers were installed on the stage.

1999
Fifth year of old dairy barn restoration. Contractors went to the roof and replaced the south face.

2000
Major reconstruction of the stage dressing rooms. Make-up rooms, showers, bathrooms, a catering room, and a production office were included in the plans.

New three-phase pedestal service and shore power for the back stage compound.

Open Exhibits building interior painted.

Sixth year of repair on the old dairy barn. The roof and the two vertical faces were completed.

The north speaker tower unit was moved farther to the north to access larger sound and lighting systems on the stage. This also centered the production on the stage with the amphitheater.

2001
North roof face of the old dairy barn replaced. The outer building is now complete at last!

Tandem loads of clay and dirt — 125 loads in all — were added to the track to increase the banks in the corners.

A major construction addition to the amphitheater began in the fall. A 160-by-16-foot enclosure at the back includes men's and women's bathrooms and showers, ticket offices, and concession areas. Plans include a central grand concourse entry into the bleacher and stadium seating areas, and into the food court. The construction includes a five-foot retaining wall and an ornamental fence the length of the project with large areas of concrete walk ways. This construction project allowed for the demolition of the obsolete old main restroom.

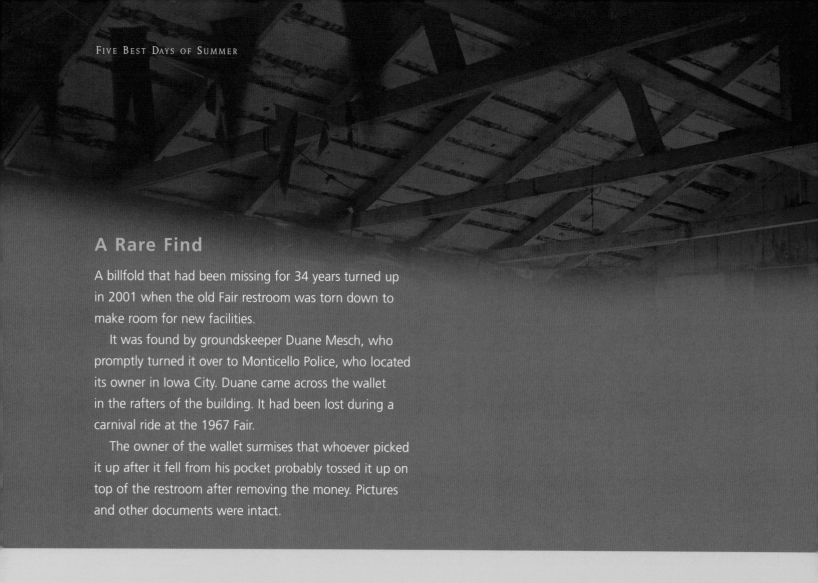

A Rare Find

A billfold that had been missing for 34 years turned up in 2001 when the old Fair restroom was torn down to make room for new facilities.

It was found by groundskeeper Duane Mesch, who promptly turned it over to Monticello Police, who located its owner in Iowa City. Duane came across the wallet in the rafters of the building. It had been lost during a carnival ride at the 1967 Fair.

The owner of the wallet surmises that whoever picked it up after it fell from his pocket probably tossed it up on top of the restroom after removing the money. Pictures and other documents were intact.

Meet the 2002 Jones County Fair Board

Front Row (left to right)
Ron Nowachek, Marilyn Streeper, Shirlee Brunsheen, Donna Robinson, Linda Kahler, Jim Hogan

Middle Row (left to right)
Merlyn Moore, John Frasher, Jack Dietiker, Dana Edwards, Russell Engelbart, Don Eilers, Marvin Manternach

Back Row (left to right)
Bob Davis, Dennis Shoop, Ryan Toenjes, Doug Monck, Dennis McDermott, Ray Poppe, Rich Kromminga, Kyle Tapken, Mike Streeper

Elected Positions

John Harms
General Manager

Andy Anderson
Concessions Manager

Joe Yedlik
Iowa State Extension Director

Dana Edwards
Executive Committee President

Russell Engelbart
Executive Committee Vice President

Pat Recker
Executive Committee Treasurer

Jani Talleen
Executive Committee Secretary

Duane Mesch
Grounds Superintendent

Mike Kraus
Plumbing

The Fair can really be an uplifting experience!

It just couldn't be a fair without a merry-go-round.

Richard Gere said to Helen Hunt, "Why don't you come down here and meet me at the Great Jones County Fair?" She came. They met. And 1,000 Eastern Iowans were with them on the Midway and in the bleachers.

PARTING SHOTS

It happened in the movie, *"Miles From Home."* Bringing in a small carnival and using skillful camera shots, the producers re-created the Fair with the help of 1,000 local "extras."

It took three all-night shoots and a lot of set-up to produce about six minutes of the movie. Filming was made more difficult by the arrival of fall's first cold snap, early in October 1987. "We had 1,000 shivering people on the sets," recalls John Harms, whose role as a bartender was limited to the appearance of one arm and the back of his head. "The kids on the rides kept their coats on until the cameras were ready, then took them off for the shoot.

"There was a big tarp behind the stands and space heaters underneath the seats. The extras in the stands would take their coats off at the last minute and sit on

them. But the hardest thing to hide was a person's breath in the cold air. You had to be careful about exhaling."

The movie, which was based on the farm recession of the mid-1980s, never clicked with audiences. It set no box office records, made no new stars. Not many people — other than those 1,000 extras in Eastern Iowa — even remember it. The fake Fair has faded.

The real Fair lives on. It is creating memories today just as it has through all the years past, filling pages in family photo albums and 4-H books, filling shelves and boxes with trophies and souvenirs. They help us remember the Fairs we enjoyed when we were young, and the Fairs our children loved so well. They help us remember parents and grandparents, and friends who have shared their lives with us.

Toto monkeying around at the Fair circa 1960.

Bell bottoms, blue ribbons, and the Fair. Michelle Jamison and Boomer in 1973.

Joal and Teagan Mackey get a ride as they eat some watermelon.

Roger Onken enjoys the Fair with grandsons Dalton, Hunter and Quintin.

The Myers family is all smiles at the 1979 Fair.

The Scherrer family in their Fair pop stand circa 1958.

ICE CREAM BAR 10¢

Lights, Camera, Action!

Before tractor pulls, there were horse-pulling contests. But in the movie, *"Miles From Home,"* a 3,000-pound ox was used. The scene was staged in the show arena of the Great Jones County Fair, with hundreds of Eastern Iowa "extras" cheering the animal's efforts.

The ox was pulling a weighted sled, obviously too heavy for its strength. A movie "bad guy" was beating the animal to make it pull harder. In the scene, the ox was supposed to collapse with a broken leg. Richard Gere, who starred in the movie, then ran into the arena and shot the animal to put it out of its misery.

Of course, the ox wasn't really killed. It didn't really break its leg. But it was really out, lying in a heap on the ground. The shot had come from a syringe, not a gun, and the vet who administered the tranquilizer had misjudged the amount needed. The overdosed ox nearly became the only casualty of the movie, lying on the ground for several hours before the drug wore off.

The movie's stars, Richard Gere and Helen Hunt, and its director, Gary Sinese, have gone on to great achievements since the 1987 filming of *"Miles From Home."* It's a safe bet that none of them has since been involved in an ox-pulling scene.

Raymond Kromminga with the Budweiser Clydesdales.

Ernie Banks

Don Hoak

Printed in U.S.A.

Eddie Mathews

Printed in U.S.A.

NEW YORK

Yogi Berra

Printed in U.S.A.

Hank Aaron

Printed in U.S.A.

MATHEWS, EDWIN
Born: Texarkana,

YEAR	CLUB
1949	H.P.-Thomsvl
1950	Atlanta
1951	Milwaukee
1952	Atlanta
1952	Boston
1953	Milwaukee
1954	Milwaukee
1955	Milwaukee
1956	Milwaukee
1957	Milwaukee
1958	Milwaukee
1959	Milwaukee
1960	Milwaukee
1961	Milwaukee
MAJOR LEA	

Big League
stars joined
Pat Lambert's
collection in
the 1960s.

Midway Treasures

When Pat Lambert was 11, he discovered the baseball card machine at the Great Jones County Fair. There were three cards – one of them Mickey Mantle – across the front. "You put a nickel in, turned a crank, and a card came out on a little tray at the bottom," he said. "That one summer, I got about 60 or 70 cards. But I never got Mickey Mantle."

Pat patronized the machine for several more summers, and he still has his cards. "I didn't put them in my bike wheels," he said. "I kept them in a cigar box. My mom never threw anything out." Dating from the early 1960s, many of them have become valuable.

Pat also credits his mom's saving ways for preserving the glass cup he won in the "dish pitch." He stuck with games that gave him a chance to take something home. "I knew right away not to go for the stuffed animals," he said.

Printed in U.S.A.

Sincerely yours Ted Williams

...ONALD ALBERT, Infielder, Pittsburgh Pirates
...oulette, Pennsylvania, Feb. 5, 1928   Ht: 6'   Wt: 175   Bats: Left   Throws: Right

Chelsea Anderson takes a spin on the merry-go-round.

Bud... weis...errr... sand sculpture, 1999

Julie Myers just loves the fish ride at the '83 Fair.

Jenny Myers takes the wheel during the 1979 Fair.

Cecilia Doyle puts a little flower, and a smile, on this youngster.

This tall turtle has a big shell and a soft spot for kids.

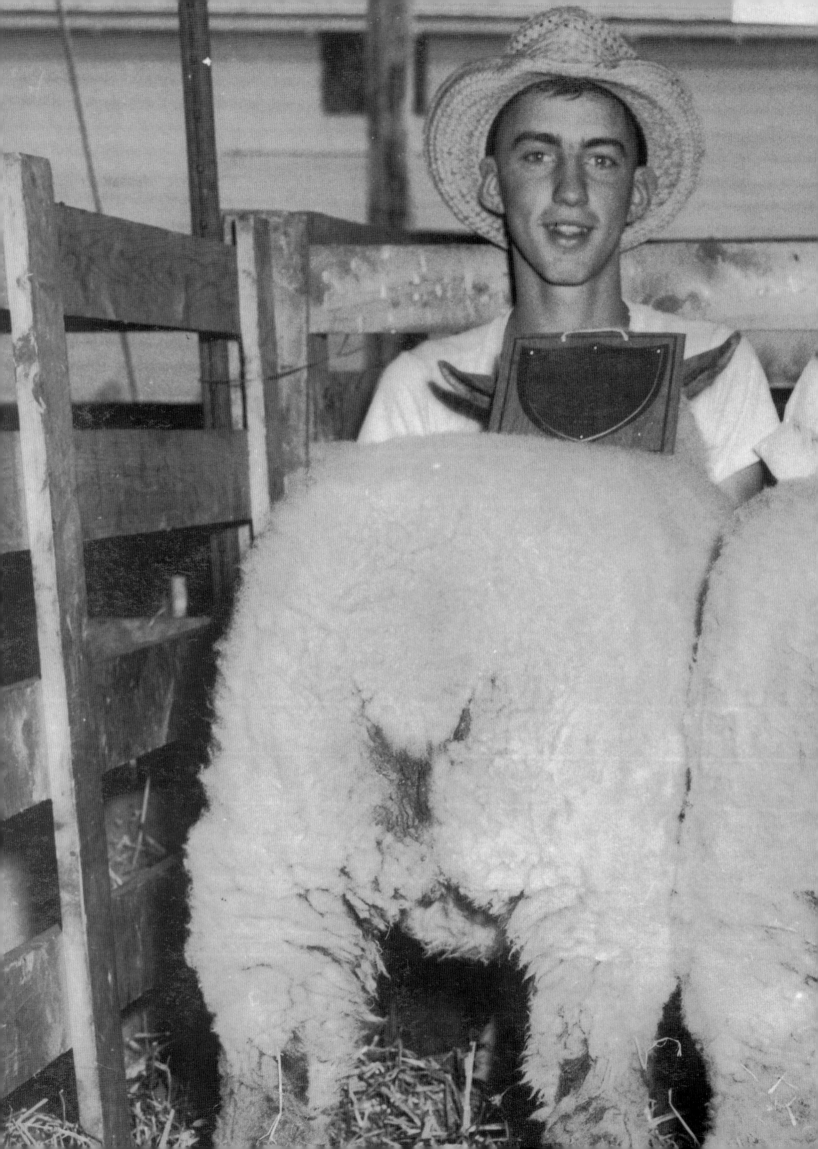

Ken Paulsen and Tom Streets with their 1956 champion pen of market lambs.

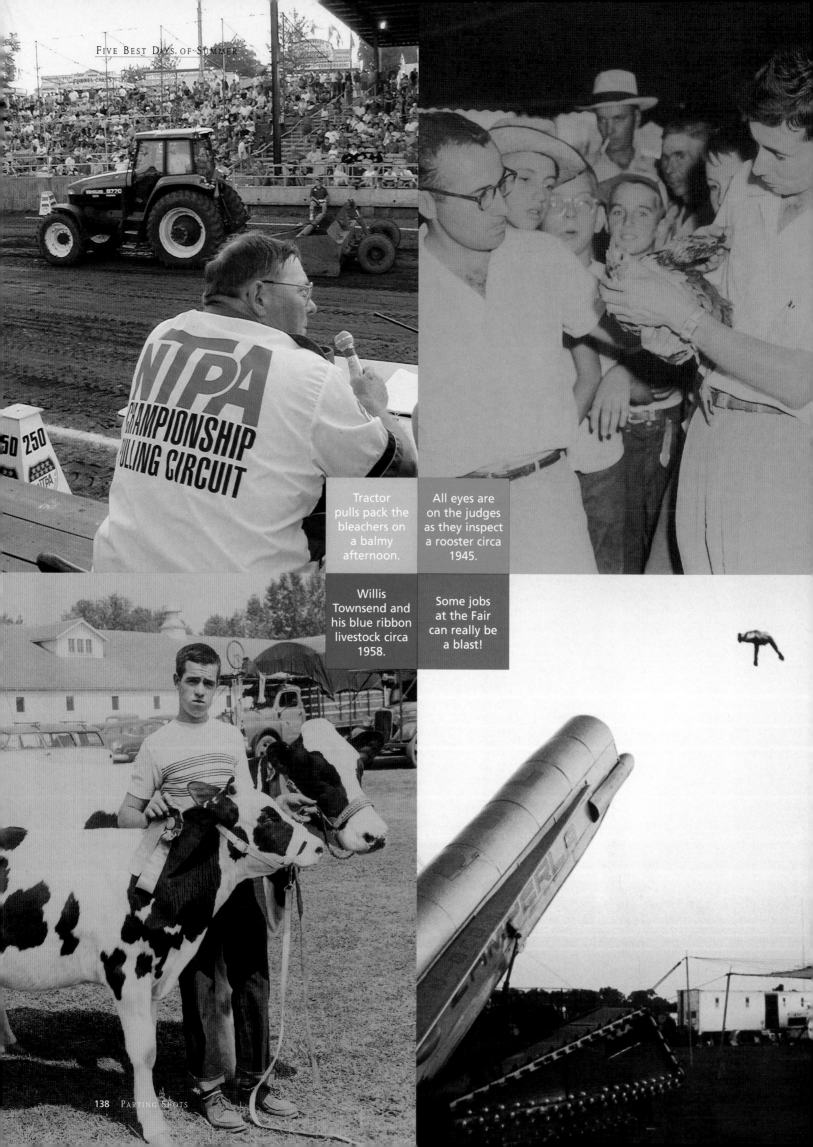

Tractor pulls pack the bleachers on a balmy afternoon.

All eyes are on the judges as they inspect a rooster circa 1945.

Willis Townsend and his blue ribbon livestock circa 1958.

Some jobs at the Fair can really be a blast!